MW00880148

EYE
LOVE
TO COOK

Prescriptions for Deliciousness

D R . G A B R I E L D E R Y

Copyright © 2021 by Dr. Gabriel Dery. 834113

All rights reserved. No part of this book may
be reproduced or transmitted in any form or by
any means, electronic or mechanical, including
photocopying, recording, or by any information storage
and retrieval system, without permission in writing from
the copyright owner.

To order additional copies of this book, contact:
Xlibris
844-714-8691
www.Xlibris.com
Orders@Xlibris.com

ISBN: Softcover   978-1-6641-0979-7
         EBook   978-1-6641-0978-0

Library of Congress Control Number: 2021920607

Print information available on the last page.

Rev. date: 10/05/2021

Dear reader,

You are extended an invitation to enjoy a journey of sights and aroma that are reminiscent of a young boy's childhood growing up in Rabat, Morocco. This was a time of great change, where political changes would transform a twelfth-century military town into a seventeenth-century haven for Barbary pirates and then into a mid-twentieth-century urban center for high-society culture, arts, and gastronomy. Whereas the cuisine of modern societies often falls prey to the passage of time, the culinary arts of Morocco remain firmly entrenched in traditions of its conquering ancestors. The Berbers introduced the tagine, a utensil from more than two thousand years ago. It allows the well-known slow-cooking practice of meats (such as khlii) using crucial ingredients essential to Moroccan cuisine, such as couscous, chickpeas, and beans. The Arabs in the seventh century introduced spices from China, India, and Malaysia, such as cinnamon, ginger, paprika, cumin, and turmeric. Influenced by the Persians, the Arabs brought nuts and dried fruits to Moroccan cuisine, blending the sweet-and-sour combination to form the foundation of many of the present tagine dishes like bastila. It is important to mention that though the recipes here are not specifically focused on Moroccan cuisine, the influences of these spices and flavors are embedded into the pages of these dishes and carry the memories of family life, friendship, gatherings, and the comfort of being back in my dear mom's kitchen of long ago.

I have love for two women who influenced me in my life—my mother, Renee Sultana, and my wife, Dr. Marina Alexandria.

Renee Sultana Dery was quite a woman, beautiful in the way that actresses of the golden age looked, but more notable was her mastery of cooking dishes from the ancient world. It was remarkable to sit in her kitchen and watch her cooking and baking for the day. She used her space in the kitchen as a canvas for her art, and we all understood that food in our family was the ultimate social agent. For years, my parents' house was open for all the family to come in and out and enjoy her cooking and patisseries at any time, during the many years I would travel from the United States of America to Morocco to visit. Watching her command the kitchen, seemingly inventing new dishes regularly, and watching her combine ingredients in certain proportions have been part of my journey that has been woven into these pages herein.

During these years, I also met my wife, Dr. Marina, who literally changed my life in the way of thinking and acting to become the person who I am now. Now that I am retired, we spend many great days cooking together. I decided to write this cooking book in memory of my mother and in the honor of my wife. I dedicate this book to both of them with all my love and appreciation.

Whether by conscious intention or a commitment to intellectual curiosity, part of this journey led to the scientific study of vision and its associated diseases. The eyes are a major sensory organ that requires special care to assure your eyesight remains keen as you age. In addition to a healthy and productive lifestyle, epidemiological, clinical, and interventional studies now recognize nutrient vision as the best method to protect your eyes from harmful reactive oxygen species, cataracts, glaucoma, age-related macular degeneration, as well as  diabetic retinopathy and hypertensive retinopathy, all leading causes of blindness in the United States.

With this in mind, many of the following recipes were designed to promote and preserve healthy eyes and contain interesting references to the latest scientific research on herbs and their connection to nutrient vision.

Dr. Gabriel Dery

Contents

I would like to thank My son Dr. Kenneth Dery, Debbie Dery and their children Sophia Hanna and Adam Abraham Dery

My son Dr. Mark Alain Dery and his wife Liana

My son Alland B Byallo for his beautiful art design of the book and who share my passion for cooking.

NOTE TO THE READERS

Before I start writing all my recipes, I would like to remind the readers that all the ingredients that I use in my recipes have a very meaningful nutritif factor(s).

All my ingredients are not only healthy for the eyes but also very nutritif for the rest of the body.

Here's a little history about herbs and spices besides the taste and an incredible job of enhancing the flavor of our food; each spice has its own chemical makeup, giving it unique properties that humans have utilized in cooking, medicine, and personal care for thousands of years.

Ancient Chinese myth suggests the medicinal use of herbs and spices began as early as 2700 BC.

Basil

The anti-inflammatory properties of basil may help lower risk of heart disease, rheumatoid arthritis, and inflammatory bowel conditions.

Oregano

Oregano herbs provide antioxidants.

Turmeric

It contains a yellow-colored chemical called curcumin, which is often used to color foods and cosmetics. Turmeric is commonly used for conditions involving pain and inflammation, such as osteoarthritis. It is also used for hay fever, depression, high cholesterol, a type of liver disease, and itching.

Thyme

Getting all the vitamins your body needs every day can be challenging. Luckily, thyme is packed with vitamin C and is also a good source of vitamin A. If you feel a cold coming on, thyme can help get you back in good health. Another health benefit of thyme is it's a good source of copper, fiber, iron, and manganese.

Cumin

Cumin contains antioxidants. Cumin seeds contain naturally occurring substances that work as antioxidants.

- Has anticancer properties
- May help treat diarrhea
- Helps control blood sugar
- Fights bacteria and parasites
- Has an anti-inflammatory effect
- May help lower cholesterol

- Aids in weight loss

Bay Leaves

1. Bay leaves are a rich source of vitamin A, vitamin C, iron, potassium, calcium, and magnesium.

2. They have been proven to be useful in the treatment of migraines.

3. Bay leaf contains enzymes that help to break down proteins and digest food faster, helping to calm indigestion.

Tomatoes

Tomatoes are the major dietary source of the antioxidant lycopene, which has been linked to many health benefits, including reduced risk of heart disease and cancer. They are also a great source of vitamin C, potassium, folate, and vitamin K.

Paprika

This helps in healing wounds.

- Treats skin problems

- Supports healthy digestion

- Prevents hair loss

- Helps maintain hair color

- Induces sleep

- Decreases the risk of heart attack

- Has anti-inflammatory properties

Rosemary

Rosemary is a rich source of antioxidants and anti-inflammatory compounds, which are thought to help boost the immune system and improve blood circulation.

- Rosemary is considered a cognitive stimulant and can help improve memory performance and quality.

Garlic

It has been used commonly by ancient Greeks and Romans.

One of the best superfoods in terms of nutritional values.

One clove of garlic contains manganese, vitamin B6, vitamin C, selenium fiber, calcium, potassium, copper, phosphorus, iron, and vitamin B1.

Garlic can combat different illnesses, including common cold; reduce blood pressure; and improve cholesterol level.

Garlic contains antioxidants that may prevent Alzheimer's disease and dementia.

EGGPLANT

It is a fat-free vegetable. It is low-glycemic food, which is good for people with diabetes. It contains manganese that helps to maintain healthy bones.

Many other nutrients contained in eggplant and specifically in its skin contribute to healthy digestion and reduce the rate of cardiovascular disease and cancer.

SAFFRON

Apart from having a unique color and flavor, saffron is rich in vitamin A, folic acid, riboflavin, niacin, and vitamin C.

ONION

Onions contain a decent amount of vitamin C, folate (B9), vitamin B6, and potassium.

CORIANDER/CILANTRO

Fresh coriander leaves are a wonderful source of dietary fiber, manganese, iron, magnesium, vitamin C, vitamin K, and protein. You could also find a small amount of calcium, phosphorus, potassium, thiamin, niacin, and carotene. It has been proven to be beneficial for improving blood sugar levels.

There are many more herbs and spices that I have not mentioned in this book. The list would be too long. I have mentioned only the herbs and spice that I use in my cooking.

APPETIZERS

POMEGRANATE SYRUP OR MOLASSES

INGREDIENTS

4 cups pomegranate juice
½ cup sugar
1 tablespoon freshly squeezed lemon juice

PREPARATION

For syrup: Place the pomegranate juice, sugar, and lemon juice in a 4-quart saucepan set over medium heat. Cook, stirring occasionally, until the sugar has completely dissolved. Once the sugar has dissolved, reduce the heat to medium-low and cook until the mixture has reduced to 1½ cups, approximately 50 minutes. It should be the consistency of syrup. Remove from the heat and allow to cool in the saucepan for 30 minutes. Transfer to a glass jar and allow to cool completely before covering and storing in the refrigerator for up to 6 months.

For molasses: Place the pomegranate juice, sugar, and lemon juice in a 4-quart saucepan set over medium heat. Cook, stirring occasionally until the sugar has completely dissolved. Once the sugar has dissolved, reduce the heat to medium-low and cook until the mixture has reduced to 1 cup, approximately 70 minutes. It should be the consistency of a thick syrup. Remove from the heat and allow to cool in the saucepan for 30 minutes. Transfer to a glass jar and allow to cool completely before covering and storing in the refrigerator for up to 6 months.

BAHARAT

2 teaspoons smoked paprika

2 teaspoons ground cumin

1 teaspoon freshly ground black pepper

1 teaspoon ground coriander

½ teaspoon ground cinnamon

½ teaspoon ground nutmeg

¼ teaspoon ground cardamom

¼ teaspoon ground cloves

Enjoy this delicious dish.

CHICKEN LIVER PÂTÉ

½ pound chicken livers, well trimmed
½ small onion, thinly sliced
1 small garlic clove, smashed and peeled
1 bay leaf
¼ teaspoon thyme leaves
kosher salt
½ cup water
1½ sticks unsalted butter, at room temperature
2 teaspoons cognac or scotch whiskey
freshly ground pepper
toasted baguette slices, for serving

PREPARATION

In a medium saucepan, combine the chicken livers, onion, garlic, bay leaf, thyme, and ½ teaspoon of salt. Add the water and bring to a simmer. Cover, reduce the heat to low, and cook, stirring occasionally, until the livers are barely pink inside, about 3 minutes. Remove from the heat and let stand, covered, for 5 minutes.

Discard the bay leaf. Using a slotted spoon, transfer the livers, onion, and garlic to a food processor; process until coarsely pureed. With the machine on, add the butter, 2 tablespoons at a time, until incorporated. Add the cognac, season with salt and pepper, and process until completely smooth. Scrape the pâté into 2 or 3 large ramekins. Press a piece of plastic wrap directly onto the surface of the pâté and refrigerate until firm. Serve chilled.

Make ahead. The pâté can be covered with a thin layer of melted butter, then wrapped in plastic and refrigerated for up to 1 week or frozen for up to 2 months.

SALTED POTATOES

large sage leaves, chopped
1 teaspoon chopped rosemary
1 teaspoon thyme leaves
1 teaspoon finely grated lemon zest
1 tablespoon kosher salt
4 pounds fingerling potatoes, halved lengthwise
2 tablespoons extra-virgin olive oil
2 tablespoons unsalted butter, melted
freshly ground pepper

Preheat the oven to 425°. In a mini food processor, pulse the sage, rosemary, and thyme until finely chopped. Add the lemon zest and pulse to blend. Add the salt and pulse until finely ground. Transfer the herb salt to a small bowl.

In a large bowl, toss the potatoes with the oil and butter and season with pepper. Spread the potatoes in a single layer on 2 large rimmed baking sheets and roast for 25 minutes. Season the potatoes generously with the herb salt, toss well, and continue baking for 5 minutes or until the potatoes are tender and golden. Transfer to a bowl and serve hot or warm.

ARTICHOKE SQUARE

INGREDIENTS

1 14-ounce can artichoke hearts, not marinated, drained and chopped

1 small onion, finely chopped

1 minced garlic clove

4 eggs

¼ teaspoon each of cayenne, oregano, pepper, salt, and curry (d'habitude, je double les épices et le curry, 1 c. à thé pour plus de saveur)

¼ c. dry bread crumbs

½ pd. shredded sharp cheddar cheese

2 teaspoons minced parsley

PREPARATION

Sauté garlic and onion over medium heat for about 5 minutes. Beat eggs in bowl, and add seasonings and crumbs, cheese, and parsley. Mix in onion and garlic mixture and artichoke hearts. Press into a greased 8 × 8 pan. Bake at 325° for 35 minutes until the center is well-done.

PICKLED HERRING

It is a dish that has been served for centuries in the northern countries of Europe and Russia. To be eaten in several different ways but definitely with a shot of vodka.

2 to 4 herring fillets
¾ cup of water
¾ cup of white vinegar
1 to 2 bay leaves
2 to 4 cloves of garlic
¼ teaspoon of black peppercorns
¼ teaspoon whole spice
¼ teaspoon of dill seed
$1/3$ cup of granulated sugar
1 red onion

PREPARATION

Soak the fillets of herring in cold water in the refrigerator for 12 to 24 hours. Change the water a couple of times.

In a cooking pan, combine water, vinegar, seasonings, sugar, and bring to a boil. Stir to dissolve the sugar and then let it cool aside to make the pickling solution.

Rinse the fillets in cold water and pat dry with a paper towel.

Cut the fillets in 1-inch pieces while you remove all the bones.

Cut the onion in regular rings.

Alternate layers of onion rings and herring in sterilized jars.

Pour the pickling solution on top of the herring and close tightly.

Refrigerate for 3 to 4 days before serving it.

One way of serving it is to cut the herring in smaller pieces, mixed with lemon juice, cilantro, finely cut chives, and a teaspoon of extra-virgin olive oil, on top of a cracker and a shot of vodka.

Enjoy!

MARINATED MUSHROOMS

Here is a very simple appetizer to be served with toasted slices of French baguette.

INGREDIENTS

1 or 2 pounds of mixed brown-and-white mushrooms
4 tablespoons of good extra-virgin olive oil
3 tablespoons of wine vinegar
3 to 4 cloves of garlic, minced depending on how strong you like it
¼ cup of red onion or shallots, finely chopped
2 tablespoons of fresh oregano, finely chopped, or dry oregano
2 tablespoons of fresh thyme, finely chopped, or dry thyme
1.2 teaspoons of salt
½ teaspoon of black peppercorn
¼ teaspoon of coriander (cilantro)

PREPARATION

Wash mushrooms very well and remove the stems. Boil mushrooms in salt water for about 10 minutes, drain, and let it cool aside.

Combine all the other ingredients in a tightly closed jar and shake very well until all the ingredients are well mixed.

Add the mushroom to the jar, shake well, close tightly, and refrigerate overnight.

Remove from the refrigerator a good 10 minutes before serving it.

A good cold white Riesling wine is to be served with the appetizer.

Enjoy!

STUFFED MUSHROOMS

Here is another appetizer for mushroom lovers. Simple and easy to make.

INGREDIENTS

    1 or 2 pounds of large brown mushrooms
    1 or 2 cloves of garlic, crushed
    1 cup of fresh parsley, finely chopped
    2 tablespoons of unsalted butter
    1 teaspoon of extra-virgin olive oil
    1 cup of bread croutons already flavored, finely ground
    1 teaspoon of Dijon mustard
    Parmesan cheese

PREPARATION

Wash the mushrooms very well, remove the stems and pat dry with a paper towel.

Cut the stems very finely chopped and put in a large bowl.

Add all the other ingredients, including Parmesan cheese, and put in the microwave for 20 seconds to melt the butter. Once the butter is melted, mix very well until you get a good paste.

Fill the mushrooms with the paste, equally until none is left.

Put the filled mushrooms in a baking rack, sprinkle more Parmesan cheese, and put in the oven already heated at 400 °F for 20 minutes.

Serve as it comes out of the oven with crackers and white wine.

Enjoy!

SALMON TARTARE

This dish can be used for appetizers or for dinner, depending how hungry you are.

Either way, it can be accompanied with pink champagne to enhance the taste of the salmon.

INGREDIENTS

1 or 2 salmon steaks (depending if it is for appetizer or dinner)
2 or 3 slices of smoked salmon
Half a lime juice
1 cup of chives, well chopped
1 cup of cilantro, well chopped

PREPARATION

Cut the salmon steaks into small pieces and put into a big bowl, then add the smoked salmon, cut into small pieces as well.

Add the lime juice, the chopped chives, and the chopped cilantro.

Mix very well and refrigerate until being served.

Serve chilled with toasted slices of French baguette or crackers accompanied with pink champagne to enhance the taste.

Enjoy!

GARLIC CHIVE STIR-FRY

As a sauce that you can enjoy with any dish, it gives the food a great flavor.

INGREDIENTS

2 to 3 bunches of chives (I usually get them from my garden.)
1 to 2 tablespoons of soy sauce (You can also use light soy sauce.)
2 tablespoons of chicken or water if you do not have any chicken broth
½ teaspoon of sugar
1 teaspoon of virgin olive oil (or you can use any other oil for stir-frying)
1 teaspoon of cornstarch mixed with 4 teaspoons of water

PREPARATION

Wash very well bunches of chives and let it drain. Cut in 1- to 2-inch pieces.

Combine the soy sauce, chicken broth, and sugar. Set aside.

Heat wok and oil over medium-high heat. When oil is hot, add the cut chives. Stir-fry for about one minute until they get brighter green.

Add the cornstarch water and mix with the stir-fried chives, stirring quickly very well to get a thicker mixture until the sauce is boiling without overcooking it.

You can use this sauce over any dish that you wish to eat or over some steamed vegetables. It gives it a very good taste.

Enjoy!

SCRAMBLED EGGS

It is a dish that you can have either for breakfast or for lunch. It is very tasty to accompany this dish with toasted bread of your choice. I like French baguette cut in slices.

INGREDIENTS

1 to 2 garlic cloves, minced very finely
a bunch of chives, cut in small pieces
4 large eggs or less, depending on how many are eating this dish
1½ teaspoon light soy sauce or ½ teaspoon of salt
freshly ground black or white pepper to taste
1 teaspoon olive oil
2 teaspoons vegetable or peanut oil (I usually stay with olive oil only)

PREPARATION

In a small bowl, beat the eggs very lightly. Add the soy sauce or salt and a teaspoon of oil, whichever you want to use. I use olive oil and pepper.

Heat a skillet on medium-high heat and add the remaining oil by spreading the oil all around the skillet to cover the whole skillet.

When the oil is hot, add the garlic and the chives. Stir-fry briefly, then add the egg mixture. Reduce the heat to medium and scramble the egg mixture.

Remove from heat and serve hot.

Enjoy with a glass of wine if you are having lunch or a cup of coffee if you are having breakfast.

HOW TO MAKE A GREAT PIZZA

Being in several different cruises, I learned to enjoy eating a good pizza while you are sailing in high seas and having lunch on a deck. I did several times ask the people on board to share with me their pizza recipe. And here it is.

INGREDIENTS

3 cups flour
2 teaspoons active or instant yeast
1 pinch sugar
1 to 1¼ lukewarm water
2 tablespoons virgin olive oil
1 teaspoon salt
flour for dusting
cornmeal for dusting bottom of pan

PREPARATION

If using active dry yeast, dissolve it with a pinch of sugar in 2 tablespoons of lukewarm water.

Let the yeast and water sit at room temperature for 15 minutes until the mixture has bubbled and expanded.

If using instant yeast, skip the previous step.

Add flour, olive oil, and mix again until well combined.

Add salt and mix for 5 minutes. The pizza dough should be smooth and firm.

Remove from the bowl and place it in a covered container overnight in the refrigerator.

When ready to use, remove dough from the refrigerator and divide into 2 equal pieces. Depending on how large you want to make the pizzas, shape each piece into a ball.

Spray dough with cooking oil and allow to rest at room temperature for 1 hour, covered loosely with plastic wrap.

Preheat the oven to 450 °F.

Dust a flat surface with flour. Gently press one ball into a disk shape on the floor surface.

Sprinkle dough with flour and stretch into a large round shape. Dip fingertips in flour if the dough gets sticky.

Carefully transfer dough onto a pizza pan that has been sprinkled with cornmeal to prevent sticking.

Top with sauce, mozzarella cheese, and desired toppings.

Bake in a preheated oven for 6 to 8 minutes or until the cheese and crust are golden brown.

TOMATO SAUCE FOR PIZZA

INGREDIENTS

1 28-ounce can diced tomatoes
2 cloves garlic, chopped
¼ cup olive oil
1 tablespoon dried oregano
salt and pepper to taste

PREPARATION

Heat olive oil in a large pot or skillet. Add chopped garlic and sauté lightly. Add tomatoes and bring to a boil. Reduce heat and simmer until reduced by one-third. Add dried oregano. Season to taste with salt and pepper. If you want a smoother sauce, gently use an immersion blender to the desired consistency. Allow sauce to cool before spreading on pizza dough.

I tried this recipe several times when we were back at home, and every time I tried different toppings. The ones that I enjoyed the most are pepperoni and sausages, which are previously cooked.

Enjoy with a good glass of Chianti or a good red blended wine.

EGGPLANT APPETIZER

Before Baking

1 or 2 eggplants, peeled, washed and
   sliced 1 cm
2 to 3 garlic, finely minced
1 cup of parsley, chopped very finely
2 tablespoons bread crumbs
½ lemon juice
1 tablespoon Dijon mustard
1 teaspoon dry basil
1 teaspoon dry oregano
1 teaspoon dry thyme
parmesan cheese as needed
2 wine tomatoes, sliced 1 cm
½ cup white wine
salt and pepper to taste
¼ cup olive oil

PREPARATION

Preheat the oven at 400 °F.

In a baking dish, spray some nonstick baking pan. Display the eggplant into one layer (see photo).

In a separate bowl, mix all the other ingredients and stir well until you get a thick and rich paste. With a brush, brush generously the paste to each side of the eggplant. Place a slice of tomato on top of each slice of eggplant; brush again the tomatoes with the remaining paste.

Put on top of the tomatoes generously some Parmesan cheese and place into the oven for 40 minutes.

Photo after baking. *Enjoy!*

PASTA WITH TOMATOES

This dish of pasta can be eaten for lunch if you are very hungry or for dinner with good glass of wine. You can use any pasta of your choice. I will be using penne pasta.

INGREDIENTS

1 package of pasta penne
¼ cup of whole milk (You can use also fat-free milk)
1 cup whipping cream
2 tablespoons of flour
$\frac{1}{3}$ cup of grated Parmesan cheese
1 tablespoon of olive oil
2 to 3 cloves of garlic
¼ teaspoon of crushed red pepper flakes
1 package fresh baby spinach
1 can diced tomatoes
1 teaspoon dry oregano
1 tablespoon fresh basil
salt and pepper to taste

PREPARATION

In a small pot with boiling water, cook the penne until tender.

In a small bowl, whisk together cream, milk, and Parmesan cheese. Set aside.

In a large skillet with olive oil, over medium heat, add garlic and red pepper and cook for 2 to 3 minutes, stirring constantly. Add spinach, diced tomatoes, oregano, salt, and pepper. Keep stirring and cook for another 2 to 3 minutes or until spinach begins to wilt.

Pour in cream mixture and cook until thickened, about 3 to 4 minutes, stirring constantly. Add the penne and the fresh basil.

Serve immediately with a glass of white wine.

Enjoy!

ESCARGOTS WITH BUTTER

I must admit that I love the taste of escargot with salted butter. It is easy and delicious with a glass of white wine.

INGREDIENTS

1 cup of salted melted butter
2 to 3 cloves garlic, finely chopped or crushed depending if you like garlic
½ cup of white wine
1 can of cooked escargots
½ cup of cognac of your choice or brandy
1 cup parsley, finely chopped
You must have some porcelain escargot shells and the dish to go with it.
French baguette toast

PREPARATION

In a bowl with the melted butter, add garlic, parsley, white wine, and cognac or brandy. Mix well to get a good paste.

Put the escargots inside the shells, then with a spoon, fill in the shell with the paste well packed. Keep refrigerated until ready to serve.

Preheat the oven at 425 °F and cook the escargots for 10 to 15 minutes or until you see the butter bubbling.

Serve immediately with some toast of French baguette and the same white wine. Hum! It is delicious.

Enjoy!

POBLANO SAUCE

I have found out that making an extra sauce tasty and spicy could be useful for people who like spicy food without impinging on other significant persons by forcing them to eat spicy cooked food.

INGREDIENTS

2 to 3 poblano peppers, washed and cut lengthwise
    (remove all seeds)
1 tablespoon vegetable oil
2 to 3 small crushed garlic cloves
salt to taste
1 teaspoon of cayenne

PREPARATION

Grind the peppers in very small pieces. Remove all the water that it releases and put the pepper in a regular bowl. Add the pepper, garlic, vegetable oil, and salt. Mix well and store in a jar to be refrigerated. For people who really like spicy food, add also the cayenne.

Every time you need to enhance the taste of your food to make it spicier, add a teaspoon of this delicious sauce.

Enjoy!

CURED SALMON

For those who like smoked salmon and cannot afford it, here is a fast way to make cured salmon that you can enjoy as much as smoked salmon.

INGREDIENTS

> 2 to 3 pounds fillet of fresh salmon
> 3 tablespoons salt
> 1 tablespoon sugar

PREPARATION

Wash the fillet of salmon and pat dry. Lay the fillet over a cotton cloth over a plate large enough to hold the whole fillet.

In a small bowl, mix the salt and sugar well and spray the salmon on both sides with the mixture.

Roll the cotton cloth over the salmon like making a package, well tight.

Put over the salmon a weight of 4 to 5 pounds and refrigerate for 36 hours.

Remove from the refrigerator and taste to make sure it is not too salty. If it is, rinse with cold water.

Slice as much as we wish to eat and *enjoy* it with any drink of your choice.

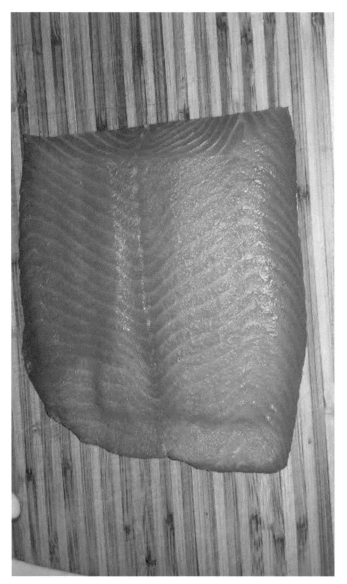

MELON WITH PROSCIUTTO

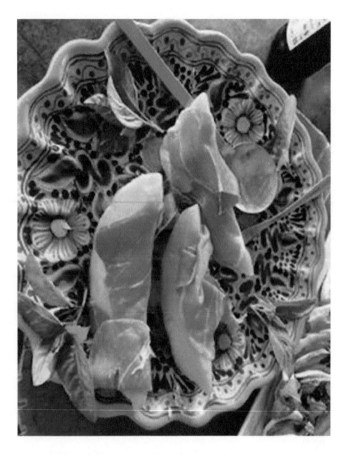

During the hot weather, it is always very nice to have a nicely chilled melon covered with a nice Italian prosciutto.

INGREDIENTS

    1 melon or cantaloupe, well ripped, cut in long slices
    1 pound of Italian prosciutto
    1 cup of squeezed lemon

PREPARATION

In a large platter, lay some greenery and place the melon covered with prosciutto.

Spray some lemon juice over and serve chilled.

It is good to eat with a glass of champagne well chilled.

Enjoy!

MELON WITH PROSCIUTTO

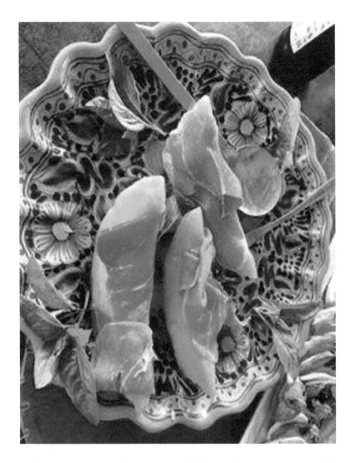

When the weather is really hot, here is a good way to cool off.

INGREDIENTS

1 large melon of your choice.
½ to 1 pound of raw prosciutto, sliced
½ cup of lemon or ½ cup of orange juice, whichever you prefer
½ tablespoon of honey if you like it sweet

PREPARATION

Cut the melon in slices and set aside in the refrigerator for 1 hour to make it cold.

In a dish, roll each slice of melon with a slice of prosciutto. Set aside until you serve it.

Before serving the melon as an appetizer, pour either the lemon juice or the orange juice over the melon by asking your guests their preference.

Mix the honey to the juice and serve it chilled with a glass of champagne.

Enjoy!

HERRING APPETIZER

Herring is very high in vitamin A, vitamin D, vitamin B12, and folate. It is also a good source of minerals, such as calcium, phosphorus, potassium, and magnesium.

If you like herring, you can make a great appetizer, and here is a quick recipe.

INGREDIENTS

> 2 to 3 fillets of herring (You can buy it at any Russian markets, or you can prepare yourself, cut into ½-inch pieces.)
> ½ cup of very finely chopped chives
> 1 tablespoon of freshly squeezed lemon juice
> 1 small clove of garlic (optional)
> 1 tablespoon of cilantro
> 1 small Brie, already well fermented
> 1 Russian black bread sliced ½-inch thick

PREPARATION

In a large bowl, mix the lemon juice, cilantro, chives, optional garlic, and the pieces of herring.

Let it simmer for 30 minutes in the refrigerator.

When ready to serve, toast the Russian bread and spread a large amount of soft Brie.

Enjoy eating the herring with the Russian bread and a glass of red wine.

Enjoy!

CURED SALMON

My cured salmon is used as smoked salmon. I make it very often and enjoy eating it with cream cheese in the morning or mixed with raw salmon and eating it as salmon tartare.

Here is my recipe.

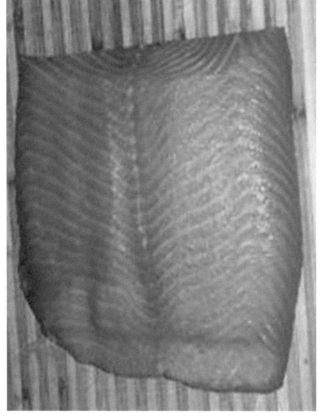

INGREDIENTS

   1 or 2 large filets of raw salmon

PREPARATION

From any fish market or any market, buy a fresh salmon fillet as per the picture.

Cut the fillet in half, put aside a half, and wash the other half with cold water. Pat dry and set aside.

In a separate bowl, pour 3 tablespoons of kosher salt and a tablespoon of ground sugar. Mix very well and spray over the dry salmon on both sides.

Cover the salmon with a cotton cloth and lay over a flat dish. Put a heavy weight on top of the salmon to cover the whole salmon and refrigerate it for 2 days.

Remove the salmon from the refrigerator and rinse the whole salmon with cold water.

Your cured salmon is ready to slice and eat. See the second picture above.

You can eat it as is or mix it for salmon tartare with raw salmon or make a good sushi with it. Serve it cold with any beverage of your choice.

Enjoy!

SALADES

TUNA SALAD

Here is a quick lunch to make if you are hungry and cannot wait. It takes only a few minutes to do it.

INGREDIENTS

a can of tuna (either in oil or in water, your preference)
1 clove garlic, well chopped
$^1/_3$ cup of parsley, well chopped
1 teaspoon of real mayonnaise (you can make it yourself, if you have time)
1 or 2 baby pickled cucumbers
½ regular cucumber, chopped very finely

PREPARATION

In a small bowl, mix all the above ingredients: tuna, pickled cucumber, cucumber, garlic, parsley, and mayonnaise. Mix very well until all ingredients are together as a paste.

Enjoy with any drink of your choice.

TUNA SALAD

A dish that you can enjoy for lunch with some crackers or French baguette.

INGREDIENTS

1 can tuna of your choice
2 large cucumbers, picked and cut in small pieces
½ cup parsley, finely chopped
1 to 2 garlic cloves
1 to 2 teaspoon of mayonnaise
½ teaspoon of ground dill

PREPARATION

In a large bowl, mix the tuna, pickled cucumber, parsley, dill, garlic, and mayonnaise.

Mix well until all ingredients are all together mixed.

Serve over crackers or French baguette.

Enjoy!

EGGPLANT SALAD

INGREDIENTS

2 large eggplants, cut in small cubes
8 garlic cloves, crushed into small pieces
1 cup of chopped cilantro (coriander)
½ teaspoon of cumin
½ teaspoon of chili pepper
½ teaspoon of black ground pepper
1 full teaspoon of sweet paprika
1 cup of water
¼ cup of white vinegar
1 bay leaf
½ cup of olive oil
salt
salade cuite

PREPARATION

In a large skillet, pour all the eggplant and add half a cup of water over a low fire. Keep stirring until the eggplant is transparent and soft.

Add all the above spices—garlic, cilantro, cumin, chili pepper, ground black pepper, paprika, bay leaf—the other half of water, salt, and olive oil.

Keep stirring until you get a good mixture.

Once you get a good thick mixture, add the salade cuite and keep cooking over a very low fire until the eggplant becomes like a jam.

Keep tasting and add salt to your liking.

It is a very good eggplant salad that you can use over a good black bread or to be used in an omelet or just as a meal.

Enjoy with a good glass of red wine.

SALADE CUITE BY MY MOTHER

(COOKED SALAD)

This recipe is quite special. It is my mother's recipe and given to me with her own handwriting. I am inserting a picture of the recipe written on an envelope. I have made it, and it is quite delicious. I grew up having this salade cuite every Friday night for Shabbat dinner.

INGREDIENTS

4 large skinless tomatoes, cut into small pieces
1 tablespoon tomato sauce
4 large bell peppers (green and red), oven roasted
1 teaspoon of crushed garlic
1 teaspoon of paprika
1 tablespoon of virgin olive oil

PREPARATION

In a large skillet, use the olive oil and paprika to sauté the garlic for a couple of minutes.

Aside, in a large bowl full of boiling water, soak the tomatoes for a minute to remove the skin easily. Cut the tomatoes in small pieces.

To the skillet, add the pieces of tomatoes with the tomato sauce and simmer for a few minutes.

Add on top of the tomatoes the bell peppers, already roasted, and cut lengthwise into strips and let cook until all the liquid has been absorbed.

Refrigerate and serve cold either as a salade or as an appetizer over toasted slices of French baguette. Crackers could also be used.

Enjoy!

CARROT SALAD BY MY MOTHER

It is a salad that was served only for Friday night dinner.

INGREDIENTS

4 to 6 fresh long carrots, peeled and cut in slices ¼ inch
2 tablespoons olive oil
1 cup cilantro/parsley
2 garlic cloves, very finely chopped
salt and pepper to taste
2 tablespoons cumin
1 tablespoon lemon juice

PREPARATION

Put the carrots in boiling water for 4 to 5 minutes until the carrots are soft when poked with a fork. Set aside to cool off.

In a bowl, pour the oil, garlic, cilantro/parsley, salt, pepper, cumin, and lemon juice. Mix well and add the carrots. Mix well again and serve on a serving platter.

These carrots can be served as an appetizer.

Enjoy!

SALADE CUITE

Green bell peppers are very high in vitamin C, vitamin K1, vitamin E, vitamin A, folate, and potassium.

Tomatoes are a major source of the antioxidant lycopene, which has been linked to many, many health benefits, including reduced risk of heart disease and cancer.

To have this recipe in your refrigerator is always good because you can always serve it as an appetizer or as a salad during a main course.

INGREDIENTS

6 to 8 tomatoes, medium-sized, already washed, peeled, and cut into small pieces

2 to 4 cloves of garlic, finely chopped

1 large or 2 medium green bell peppers, roasted, peeled, and cut in length

2 teaspoons salt

1 teaspoon ground pepper

½ cup of olive oil

PREPARATION

Preheat the oven at 350 °F.

In a large pot over medium heat, cook the olive oil, tomatoes, garlic, salt, and pepper by stirring constantly to avoid the tomatoes from sticking to the bottom of the pot. Add the roasted bell peppers to the tomatoes and cook for 30 minutes over low heat by stirring and mixing both the bell pepper and the tomatoes.

You will get a thick kind of amalgam.

Set aside and let it cool. Refrigerate when cold.

Enjoy!

SOUPS

FRENCH ONION SOUP

When you go to a French restaurant, you always have on the menu the famous onion soup. Here is a recipe that you can make yourself and enjoy with your friends, guests, and family.

INGREDIENTS

2 tablespoons unsalted butter, plus softened butter, for spreading
3 large onions (about 2 pounds), halved lengthwise and thinly sliced crosswise
sea salt
2 tablespoons dry sherry wine
1 quart of beef broth
freshly ground pepper
four ½-inch-thick slices sourdough (baguette) bread, cut into 4-inch rounds
1 bouquet: made with 1 bay leaf, 1 thyme sprig, 2 juniper berries, and 2 flat-leaf
    parsley sprigs, tied in cheesecloth
2 cups shredded Gruyère cheese (about 6 ounces)

PREPARATION

Melt the butter in a large enameled cast-iron casserole. Add the onions and a pinch of salt, cover and cook over medium heat, stirring once or twice until the onions soften, about 10 minutes. Uncover and cook over medium heat, stirring frequently, until the onions are lightly browned, about 40 minutes.

Stir in the sherry. Add the stock and bouquet garni and bring to a boil. Cover and simmer over low heat until the soup has a deep flavor, about 30 minutes. Discard the bouquet garni and season the soup with salt and pepper.

Preheat the oven to 350°. Butter the bread on both sides and place on a baking sheet. Toast the bread for 15 minutes, turning the slices halfway through, until golden and crisp but not dried out. Raise the oven temperature to 425°.

Bring the soup to a simmer, ladle it into 4 deep ovenproof bowls, and sprinkle with half of the cheese. Place a crouton in each bowl and sprinkle on the remaining cheese. Bake the bowls of soup on a baking sheet in the middle of the oven for 10 minutes or until the cheese is bubbling. Serve hot.

Make ahead. The recipe can be prepared through step 3 up to 3 days ahead.

MOROCCAN HARIRA SOUP

It is a soup that is eaten or drunk after a full day of fasting during the month of Ramadan. Jews of Morocco also used to make it during that time and drink it to be associated with the personnel that they were employed.

INGREDIENTS

8 ounce lamb, beef, or chicken, diced
3 tablespoons vegetable or olive oil
several soup bones (beef or lamb bones, optional)
2 pounds soft ripe tomatoes (about 6 large)
1 handful frozen chickpeas, already thawed
2 handfuls dry green or brown lentils, soaked overnight
1 large onion, grated
1 stalk celery with leaves chopped
1 small bunch flat-leaf parsley, finely chopped
1 small bunch cilantro, finely chopped
1 tablespoon smen (optional)
1 tablespoon salt
1 tablespoon ginger
1.5 teaspoons black pepper
1 teaspoon ground cinnamon
½ teaspoon turmeric
3 tablespoons tomato paste, combined with 2 cups water
3 tablespoons uncooked rice or broken vermicelli
1 cup flour combined with 2 cups water
lemon wedge and cilantro for garnish

Ahead of time, prep ingredients.

Pick through the lentils.

BEANS SOUP

It is a soup that could be served before a good BBQ dinner.

- 1 cup of red beans (okay in can)
- 1 cup of white beans (okay in can)
- 1 cup of fresh green beans
- 1 cup of spaghetti
- 3 large or 5 small white potatoes
- 2 medium or 1 large yellow onion
- 5 medium zucchinis
- 2 large wine tomatoes
- 4 to 5 garlic cloves
- 1 tablespoon of basil
- 1 tablespoon of virgin olive oil
- 3 or 4 stems of Italian parsley

PREPARATION

In a slow cooker, cook the red and white beans together with the onion, potatoes, zucchinis, and tomatoes. Remove the tomatoes and grind the vegetables; add the green beans and the spaghetti and cook for 30 minutes until all the vegetables are tender and soft.

In a bowl, grind the tomatoes to a puree; add basil, garlic, olive oil, and keep stirring as you were making a mayonnaise. Pour the content of the bowl into the slow cooker and let it cook in low setting for another hour.

Keep checking to make sure that the soup is not being overcooked.

Serve hot with a stem of parsley.

Enjoy!

TUNA SOUP

A soup that could be served before a dinner entirely composed of fish.

INGREDIENTS

> 2 cans tuna fish in water
> 1 can tuna fish in oil
> 1 ground large onion
> 2 fresh wine tomatoes, medium-sized
> 1 can of tomato paste
> salt and pepper to taste
> 1 bay leaf
> 1 teaspoon basil
> 1 tablespoon herbs from Provence
> $\frac{1}{3}$ teaspoon of

PREPARATION

Sauté the onion in olive oil until it becomes translucent. Add garlic, tomatoes, tomato paste, salt, pepper, 3 cans of tuna, and all the herbs. Cook until all the ingredients are well mixed together.

Serve as is, or you can add some pasta of your choice, already cooked.

Enjoy!

FISH SOUP

If you like fish, you will enjoy this recipe of soup, which is a small version of bouillabaisse.

INGREDIENTS

1 stick of celery
2 zucchinis
2 large yellow onions
2 large tomatoes without skin
2 or 3 garlic cloves
1 bay leaf
1 tablespoon of herb de Provence
salt and pepper to taste
$\frac{1}{3}$ teaspoon of saffron
3 pounds of white fish: haddock, cod, halibut, rockfish

PREPARATION

Put all the ingredients together and cook them in water, then pour in a strainer to make a bouillon.

To the bouillon, add the fish, bay leaf, and garlic. Grind roughly the whole mixture very quickly, add some water, and cook.

You could serve this soup with some cooked pasta of your choice or just as is.

A good glass of white wine will be appropriate.

Enjoy!

CABBAGE SOUP

This is my wife, Marina's, favorite soup and also a recipe. I am inserting it in my book because the last few times, I am the one who cooked it and rearranged the flavor.

If you want to be on a diet, this soup, as a full meal, will make you quite comfortable and shed some weight.

INGREDIENTS

    1 full cabbage, shredded in small pieces
    2 cloves garlic
    5 broccoli florets
    5 large spinach leaves
    2 bay leaves
    2 large wine tomatoes, peeled and cut in small cubes
    1 can diced tomatoes
    1 pinch pepper
    1 pinch salt
    2 to 3 large carrots, peeled and round-cut 1 inch
    1 cup frozen peas
    1 cup parsley
    1 cup dill

PREPARATION

Over high heat, boil water in a large cooking pan. Once the water is boiled, reduce the heat to medium and add diced tomatoes and cubed tomatoes. Stir well to mix the tomatoes for 2 to 3 minutes. Add garlic, broccoli, spinach, bay leaves, carrots, frozen peas, salt, and pepper. Let it cook for 5 minutes in reduced heat. Add the shredded cabbage, dill, and parsley to the soup and cook for another 5 minutes. Taste for flavor and add any salt or pepper to your taste.

Serve hot.

Enjoy!

LENTILS SOUP

Here is a soup complete with all vitamins and delicious for a hungry person.

INGREDIENTS

1 cup of lentils, washed and cleaned

2 cups of cold water

2 to 3 large brown mushrooms

1 cup chopped chives

4 strips turkey bacon (optional; you can cook it without turkey bacon)

1 tablespoon thyme

1 tablespoon ground basil

1 cup chopped fresh parsley

1 small bunch fresh rosemary

1 cup fresh basil

1 teaspoon ground pepper

1 teaspoon salt

3 cloves garlic, cut in half lengthwise

2 large bay leaves

PREPARATION

In a medium-sized cooking pot, pour the lentils, water, and bring to a boil.

Reduce the heat to low, add all the above ingredients, and mix well.

Keep stirring while cooking.

The lentil soup is ready when the lentils are soft.

Serve hot and *enjoy!*

FISH

MAMA'S FISH BALLS

I remember eating fish balls every Friday night as it was the custom to eat fish every Friday night at dinner. Frankly, as a youngster, we did not care too much, but as I recall now, it was a feast. Now it is my turn to make this dish that everyone can enjoy with a glass of white wine.

INGREDIENTS

1 kilogram whiting fillet, cut in small pieces
½ onion, chopped finely
1 cup chopped parsley
1 egg
2 tablespoons bread crumbs
1 can of tomato coulis (1 garlic clove, 3 tablespoons olive oil, 5 bay leaves, pinched and crushed pepper, kosher salt, and freshly ground black pepper)
1 orange, zest
1 garlic clove, chopped finely
1 green pepper, cut in thin strips
salt and pepper to taste
paprika to taste
olive oil
nutmeg to taste

PREPARATION

Salt your whiting, then chop the fish and half of the onion.

Mix the fish, parsley, egg white, bread crumbs, and nutmeg in a bowl and let stand. Prepare in a pot your sauce by pouring the tomato coulis, the garlic (in pieces), and the pepper (in thin strips). Add a teaspoon of paprika, half a glass of olive oil, and bring to a boil.

Form balls of your fish stuffing the size of a walnut, and simmer for half an hour. Occasionally shake the contents, covering with sauce. If you like spicy, I recommend 2 spicy red peppers in the sauce.

Enjoy!

FRESH TUNA IN TOMATO SAUCE

INGREDIENTS

    10 to 12 medium-sized tomatoes or 2 large cans of tomato sauce
    3 to 4 garlic cloves
    1 or 2 bay leaves
    salt and pepper to taste
    2 teaspoons of brown sugar
    4 tablespoons of olive oil
    3 to 4 fresh tuna steaks or fillets
    half a cup of chopped parsley

PREPARATION

In a large skillet, cut or crush half of the garlic, add half of the olive oil, and cook over medium heat until the garlic starts to brown. *Do not burn it.*

Add the tomato sauce, bay leaves, salt, and pepper and cook for 30 minutes until the sauce is thickened. Make sure to stir the tomato sauce continuously not to stick to the skillet.

If you prefer to use the fresh tomatoes, pour boiling water over the tomatoes to remove the skin, cut in pieces, and cook over low heat. Add half of the crushed garlic, salt and pepper, and bay leaves and cook until you get a thick sauce. Stir continuously.

Remove the tomato sauce and let it stand aside.

In a different skillet, brown the other half of the crushed garlic, the other half of olive oil over medium heat, add the tuna steaks or fillets, and cook it about 3 minutes or less on each side just to brown the tuna. *Do not cook it through and through.* Leave it raw or medium raw on the inside.

To the tomato sauce, add the cooked fish, making sure that it is totally covered by the sauce. Add the brown sugar to compensate for the acidity of the tomatoes, and cook for about 3 to 4 minutes over a medium heat.

Remove from heat and serve accompanied with brown or white rice. Make sure you cover the fish with the tomato sauce and sprinkle some parsley to add some color.

Enjoy!

FRESH TUNA SEARED IN SOY SAUCE

INGREDIENTS

bottle of soy sauce
fresh tuna
parsley, finely chopped
3 tablespoons of olive oil

PREPARATION

Cut the tuna 1 inch thick by 3 to 4 inches long.

In a regular bowl, pour the soy sauce enough to cover the tuna steaks and let marinate for 2 to 3 hours in the refrigerator, *not longer*.

In a large skillet, pour the olive oil over a high heat until the oil is very hot, lower the heat to medium heat, add the tuna, and cook it on each side for about 1 to 2 minutes, making sure that the center of the tuna is still raw.

Serve the seared tuna with white or brown rice and sprinkle the parsley over the tuna. To be accompanied with a sauvignon blanc.

Enjoy!

SALMON À LA MUSTARD

INGREDIENTS

    3 or 4 salmon steaks, washed and pat dry
    2 teaspoons Dijon mustard
    2 garlic cloves
    ½ cup of chopped coriander
    salt and pepper to taste
    3 teaspoons olive oil
    1 lemon juice or lime

PREPARATION

In a separate bowl, mix Dijon mustard, crushed garlic, lemon juice, salt and pepper, chopped coriander, and 2 teaspoons of olive oil. Add the salmon steak and marinate for 1 hour.

In a large skillet, over medium-high heat, pour the remaining 1 teaspoon of olive oil, and add the salmon steak. Cook over medium heat until each side of the salmon is brown. Do not overcook the salmon. It must be served seared. Garnish with some remaining coriander and serve accompanied with pasta or baked potatoes. Do not forget to serve with a dry chardonnay to your liking.

Enjoy!

SEA BASS MOROCCAN STYLE

The marinade consists of a combination of garlic, olive oil, paprika, lemon juice, fresh mint, salt, pepper, and cumin. Some people like it spicier by adding a little cayenne pepper instead of regular white pepper for a more intense flavor.

INGREDIENTS

2 to 4 tablespoons of olive oil
1 lemon juice
2 teaspoons paprika
½ teaspoon cayenne pepper
2 to 3 cloves of garlic, finely minced
1 teaspoon cumin
½ cup cilantro, well chopped
½ cup of chopped fresh mint
2 to 3 wine tomatoes, sliced
1 red onion, sliced
salt and pepper

PREPARATION

Preheat the oven at 350 °F or light the barbecue 15 minutes before cooking.

If you are going to use the oven, in a baking dish, spray with nonstick cooking PAM and lay the fish inside. Make some skewed incisions on the fish on both sides.

Brush the fish the marinade inside and out, making sure that the marinade has penetrated the fish very well. Put the baking dish in the oven for 30 minutes, making sure that you turn the fish several times.

If you will BBQ the fish, lay the fish over a metallic foil, which has been sprayed with PAM. Brush the fish in the same manner as you did for the oven, with the skewed incisions. Place the metallic foil over the grill and cook the fish by rotating it often.

Keep brushing the fish with the remaining marinade.

Serve the fish garnished with sliced tomatoes and sliced onion salad.

Enjoy with a glass of dark beer.

ROCKFISH WITH POTATOES À LA GABRIEL

As you know, fish does not have to be cooked for a long time. Just a few minutes on each side, and it is ready to be eaten. The potatoes need to be prepared in advance and ready to be served when you add to it at the last minute the fish to pick up the flavor of the potatoes.

INGREDIENTS

4 to 6 white or red potatoes, peeled and sliced
4 to 6 fillets of rockfish, well washed and cleaned
2 cloves of garlic, well minced
½ yellow onion, finely chopped
½ cup of parsley or cilantro, whichever you have
    ready, well chopped
salt and pepper to taste
½ cup olive oil
1 teaspoon basil
1 teaspoon oregano
1 teaspoon thyme
1 teaspoon dill
½ cup sun-dried tomatoes
1 cup of white dry wine

PREPARATION

In a large skillet, put the garlic, parsley or cilantro, salt, pepper, onion, and olive oil and cook over a medium heat until the onion is translucent. Add to the skillet basil, oregano, thyme, dill, and sun-dried tomatoes and mix well.

Arrange the potatoes in a circular manner to cover the whole skillet over the sauce. Cover and cook the potatoes until tender. Taste the sauce and potatoes to add any of the above herbs.

In a separate bowl, marinate the fillets of fish in the white wine until ready to be cooked.

Just before serving dinner, arrange the fillets of fish over the potatoes, pour the white wine into the skillet, and cook each side of the fish for a few minutes only. Let it simmer just enough for the wine sauce to evaporate.

If you like mushrooms, you can add them at the last minute to enhance the taste.

Enjoy with a good glass of white wine.

RED SNAPPER À LA GABRIEL

If you ever have a chance to encounter red snapper while you are grocery shopping, make sure to grab a couple or more depending on how many people you need to feed. In the oven, baked the proper way, it is a delicatessen. Of course, accompany with a glass of great white dry wine.

INGREDIENTS

2 red snappers, scaled and cleaned by removing the fins and head
4 to 6 red potatoes, peeled and sliced
½ cup of virgin olive oil
2 to 4 garlic, finely minced
1 teaspoon thyme
1 teaspoon basil or fresh basil, finely chopped
1 teaspoon sweet paprika
salt and pepper to taste
1 squeezed lemon juice
2 wine tomatoes, sliced
1 cup cilantro, finely chopped
1 tablespoon Dijon mustard
2 to 3 chives, finely cut into small pieces with scissors
1 cup dry white wine

PREPARATION

Preheat the oven at 350 °F.

In a large baking dish, spray with cooking nonstick PAM, including the side of the baking dish.

Lay down the potatoes to cover the whole baking dish. Set aside.

In a separate bowl, pour the olive oil, garlic, cilantro, mustard, basil, thyme, salt, pepper, paprika, lemon juice, white wine, and stir well until you get a paste. If the paste is too thick, add some oil to loosen it. Taste the sauce and add whichever ingredients you need to make to your taste.

With a brush, paint the potatoes with the paste until well covered. Lay on top the 2 red snappers and paint the fish, inside and outside on both sides, with the same paste until well covered. On top of the fish, lay the sliced tomatoes to cover the whole fish and inside the fish.

Cover with foil paper and put in the oven for 35 minutes.

Take the baking dish out of the oven, remove the foil paper, and lay over the whole dish, including the fish with the cut chives.

Turn the oven off and put the dish in the oven to keep it warm until you serve it.

Enjoy with a good glass of white wine.

BAKED ROCKFISH

If you like fish, this is an easy recipe to enjoy for dinner accompanied with a tomato and cucumber salad.

INGREDIENTS

4 fillets of fresh rockfish, washed and drained
1 cup fresh parsley, finely chopped
2 to 3 garlic cloves
½ tablespoon olive oil
1.2 teaspoon ground dill
½ teaspoon basil
salt and pepper to taste
1 cup Pinot Grigio white wine

PREPARATION

In a large skillet, pour olive oil, garlic, basil, salt, pepper, dill, parsley, and wine over medium heat. Sauté the garlic and mix well with the other ingredients. Reduce the heat to low and add the fish and let simmer. Make sure to keep watering the fish with the sauce.

Serve hot with a glass of Pinot Grigio.

Enjoy!

FISH COD WITH POTATOES AND ZUCCHINIS

Here is a recipe that you can enjoy and is very fast to make. This is for the fish lovers.

INGREDIENTS

3 or 4 fillets of fish, washed and
    pat dry
1 large tomato, cut in small pieces
2 or 3 finely chopped cloves of garlic
½ cup olive oil
1 tablespoon basil
1 tablespoon oregano
1 teaspoon thyme
salt and pepper to taste
2 or 3 zucchinis, cut in ¼-inch slices
1 cup of chopped chives
2 or 3 medium round potatoes
1 cup of Pinot Grigio

PREPARATION

In a large skillet, over medium heat, mix olive oil, chives, garlic, oregano, basil, thyme, salt, and pepper. Mix well while being sautéed. Add tomato, zucchini, and potato until soft. Add the Pinot Grigio and mix well the sauce until the wine has evaporated.

10 to 15 minutes before serving, add to the skillet the fillets of fish and cook under a very low heat. Keep turning and spraying the fish with the entire sauce.

Serve hot with a glass of Pinot Grigio.

Enjoy!

ROCKFISH WITH ZUCCHINI

If you like fish, here is another quick recipe, easy and very delicious.

INGREDIENTS

> 3 to 4 fillets of fresh rockfish, washed and pat dry
> 2 to 3 zucchinis, cut in length and small wedges
> 2 to 3 finely chopped cloves of garlic
> 1 bay leaf
> 1 tablespoon of ground dill
> 1 teaspoon ground basil
> ¼ cup of olive oil
> ½ cup of finely chopped chives
> ½ cup of dry white wine of your choice

PREPARATION

In a large skillet over medium heat, mix all the above ingredients—chives, garlic, bay leaf, basil, olive oil, and dill—and cook until well mixed.

Add the zucchinis and dry wine. Simmer until the wine has evaporated. Mix well.

Nineteen to 15 minutes before serving, add to the skillet the fillets of fish. Make sure to turn it over a couple of times and spray it with the sauce.

Serve hot with a glass of the same wine you cooked it with.

Enjoy!

ROCKFISH WITH ZUCCHINIS

Fish is always good with any vegetable. This is a recipe that you can make with fresh zucchinis.

INGREDIENTS

3 to 6 fillets of rockfish or any other fish of your liking (I like the consistency of
the rockfish; wash and pat dry)
2 to 3 garlic cloves
1.2 cups of olive oil
½ cup of chopped cilantro
salt and pepper
1 to 2 fresh zucchinis, cut in slices
½ cup lemon juice

PREPARATION

In a large skillet, heat the olive oil and add garlic, salt and pepper to taste, chopped cilantro, and cook over medium heat until the garlic is well roasted.

In a separate bowl, pour some olive oil, some crushed garlic, some chopped cilantro, lemon juice, and add the fish. Set aside to marinate for 15 minutes.

Add the fish to the skillet and cook the fish by returning it once for 10 minutes.

Serve hot and with white wine of your choice.

Enjoy!

POULTRY

GRILLED CHICKEN MEXICAN WAY

This is a very flavored chicken. A bit spicy but quite good to enjoy with either a glass of cold white wine or a good dark beer. This is to remind you that we lived in Mexico for six years.

INGREDIENTS

8 chicken thighs or 4 chicken breast halves, on the bone

MARINADE INGREDIENTS

½ onion, minced
1 large garlic clove, crushed
¼ cup olive oil
½ teaspoon Mexican oregano or any oregano
½ teaspoon cumin
1 teaspoon salt
½ teaspoon black pepper
¼ teaspoon dried chipotle powder that you can find in any grocery store
1 teaspoon paprika, the sweet one is better
1 lime, juice of or 2 tablespoons apple cider vinegar
1 handful cilantro leaf (optional)

PREPARATION

Put all marinade ingredients in the blender or food processor and liquefy.

Put marinade in a gallon-size ziplock bag and add chicken pieces. Turn a few times to distribute marinade.

Refrigerate for at least 2 hours. I leave it for about 10 hours.

Remove chicken from marinade and place on a hot grill. Discard marinade.

Grill, turning occasionally, until chicken is cooked through.

Serve as soon as it comes out from the grill.

Enjoy!

HONEY-AND-LEMON–GLAZED ROAST

Chicken

If you like chicken, which I do very much, this recipe will make you wonder how good you can achieve a good meal with just some pieces of chicken to your liking. It can be any part of the chicken. I personally prefer thighs.

INGREDIENTS

three 3-pound chickens
¼ cup plus 1 teaspoon honey
2 tablespoons plus 1 teaspoon fresh lemon juice
2 tablespoons soy sauce
salt
9 large rosemary sprigs
9 garlic cloves, quartered
1 lemon, cut into 12 wedges

PREPARATION

Preheat the oven to 450°. In a small bowl, combine the honey, lemon juice, and soy sauce.

Set the chickens on a large rimmed baking sheet and tuck the wing tips underneath.

Season the cavities with salt and stuff each one with 3 rosemary sprigs, 3 quartered garlic cloves, and 4 lemon wedges. Brush two-thirds of the honey glaze over the chickens and season lightly with salt. Roast in the middle of the oven for 30 minutes.

Reduce the oven temperature to 325°. Rotate the chickens in the pan and brush with the remaining glaze. Roast the chickens for about 45 minutes longer until the juices run clear when the thighs are pierced; turn the pan halfway through roasting.

Transfer the chickens to a carving board and let rest for 15 minutes. Carve the chickens and serve.

ROASTED CHICKEN THIGHS WITH RICE

This is a fast meal to prepare and enjoy.

INGREDIENTS

4 to 6 thighs without bone
3 tablespoons olive oil
2 large garlic cloves, crushed
1 teaspoon of cumin
1 teaspoon of thyme
2 tablespoons of apple vinegar
salt and pepper to taste
1 teaspoon basil
½ lemon juice
2 tablespoons Dijon mustard
1 cup of brown rice

PREPARATION

Wash and let dry the chicken thighs.

In a large bowl, pour the olive oil, basil, crushed garlic, cumin, thyme, apple vinegar, salt, pepper, lemon juice, and Dijon mustard. Mix well and add the chicken thighs to be well marinated. Let stand for 2 hours in the refrigerator.

In a small oven, warm up the oven to broil and place the thighs flat on an oven sheet covered with foil paper. Cook for 20 minutes by turning the thighs regularly until well browned on each side.

In a small pot with boiling water, pour the rice and boil at medium heat until the water has completely evaporated. Put the rice into a skillet with some olive oil, salt, pepper, basil, thyme, and cook the rice until very tender and tasty.

Serve with rice or fresh salad (tomatoes, cucumbers, and red bell peppers) and decorate with fresh mint, accompanied with red or white wine to your choice.

Enjoy!

ROASTED WHOLE CHICKEN WITH ROSEMARY

INGREDIENTS

1 whole chicken, washed and dry
4 large crushed garlic clove
3 teaspoons Dijon mustard
1 large lemon or lime juice
salt and pepper to taste
4 or 5 rosemary spouts
1 cup of dry white wine
3 or 4 teaspoons of olive oil
5 or 6 carrots, sliced
3 large potatoes, sliced
2 large yellow, green, and red bell pepper, cut lengthwise
1 large red onion
1 teaspoon of oyster sauce

PREPARATION

Preheat the oven at 350 °F.

In a large bowl, mix all the above ingredients until you get a thick marinade.

Prepare the chicken by separating the skin and fill the space with the marinade. Rub the entire chicken with the marinade and fill the cavity with half the red onion.

In an oven-safe dish, lay down the peeled and sliced potatoes, add the peeled and sliced carrots, and add the bell peppers and the other half of the red onion.

Lay the chicken on top of the vegetables covered with foil paper and put in the oven for 60 minutes.

Uncover the chicken, remove from the dish, and let rest for 1 hour.

In a large skillet, pour all the cooked vegetables, add the white wine, a teaspoon of oyster sauce, and simmer over medium heat to taste.

Return the chicken to the oven-safe dish and broil it for another 30 minutes until brown all over.

Lay the chicken in a large plate and surround it with all the cooked vegetables. Do not forget to serve it with a very dry white wine of your choice.

Enjoy!

CHICKEN STEW

Sometimes you want to change the way you prepare your chicken.

Are you tired of roasted chicken?

Are you tired of grilled chicken?

Here is a wonderful way to prepare your chicken using nothing but organic vegetables.

INGREDIENTS

5 or 6 large chicken thighs
1 large yellow onion, finely chopped
2 good-sized carrots, peeled and cut in slices
2 large potatoes, peeled and sliced in circle of about ¼ an inch
1 cup of finely chopped cilantro
2 large garlic cloves, finely chopped
1 large bell pepper (green or yellow or red, I use yellow for the color)
1 large green poblano pepper
1 15-ounce can of cut organic tomatoes
1 15-ounce can of organic tomato sauce
1 large bay leaf or 2 small ones
1 teaspoon of paprika (I use sweet paprika from Hungary)
1 teaspoon of Montreal chicken
1 teaspoon of garlic salt
1 teaspoon of ground oregano
1 teaspoon of ground basil
1 teaspoon of ground thyme
½ teaspoon of ground pepper

PREPARATION

In a large nonstick skillet, pour the 2 cans of tomatoes, including their juice, and cook at very low fire until the tomato sauce and the cut tomatoes are well mixed. Keep the skillet cover.

Add the carrots and the potatoes well embedded in the sauce and cook until the potatoes and carrots are soft.

Add all the spices (paprika, Montreal chicken, oregano, basil, thyme, ground pepper) and stir with a wooden spoon all the spices together with the tomatoes. Let it simmer for a good 30 minutes until the mixture thickens. Keep the skillet cover.

Add the cut onion, garlic, bay leaves, and cilantro; stir to get a good amalgam and let it simmer for another 30 minutes. Keep stirring often enough to keep it well mixed.

Prepare the chicken thighs as follows:

Remove all fat and trim as lean as possible.

Cut the chicken in strips of ½ inches wide.

Wash in cold water and pat dry.

Add the chicken strips on top of the prepared sauce and cook for another 30 minutes over a very low fire, still covered.

When the chicken appears to be cooked, stir it and mix it with the sauce. Keep the skillet uncovered.

If you wish, you could add some sauvignon blanc wine, about a cup, and cook uncovered until it is no longer watery.

Serve it warm or hot accompanied with a glass of the same sauvignon blanc.

CHICKEN STEW WITH POTATOES

Sometimes you want to change the way you prepare your chicken.

Are you tired of roasted chicken?

Are you tired of grilled chicken?

Here is a wonderful way to prepare your chicken using nothing but organic vegetables.

INGREDIENTS

5 or 6 large chicken thighs
1 large yellow onion, finely chopped
2 good-sized carrots, peeled and cut in slices
2 large potatoes, peeled and sliced in circle of about ¼ of an inch
1 cup of finely chopped cilantro
2 large garlic cloves, finely chopped
1 large bell pepper (green or yellow or red, I use yellow for the color)
1 large green poblano pepper
1 15-ounce can of cut organic tomatoes
1 15-ounce can of organic tomato sauce
1 large bay leaf or 2 small ones
1 teaspoon of paprika (I use sweet paprika from Hungary)
1 teaspoon of Montreal chicken
1 teaspoon of garlic salt
1 teaspoon of ground oregano
1 teaspoon of ground basil
1 teaspoon of ground thyme
½ teaspoon of ground pepper

PREPARATION

In a large nonstick skillet, pour the 2 cans of tomatoes, including their juice, and cook at very low fire until the tomato sauce and the cut tomatoes are well mixed. Keep the skillet covered.

Add the carrots and the potatoes well embedded in the sauce and cook until the potatoes and carrots are soft.

Add all the spices (paprika, Montreal chicken, oregano, basil, thyme, ground pepper) and stir with a wooden spoon all the spices together with the tomatoes. Let it simmer for a good 30 minutes until the mixture thickens. Keep the skillet covered.

Add the cut onion, garlic, bay leaves, and cilantro; stir to get a good amalgam and let it simmer for another 30 minutes. Keep stirring often enough to keep it well mixed.

Prepare the chicken thighs as follows:

Remove all fat and trim as lean as possible.

Cut the chicken in strips of ½-inch wide.

Wash in cold water and pat dry.

Add the chicken strips on top of the prepared sauce and cook for another 30 minutes over a very low fire, still covered.

When the chicken appears to be cooked, stir it and mix it with the sauce. Keep the skillet uncovered.

If you wish, you could add some sauvignon blanc wine, about a cup, and cook uncovered until it is no longer watery.

Serve it warm or hot accompanied with a glass of the same sauvignon blanc.

CHICKEN WITH BROWN RICE AND SAUSAGE

INGREDIENTS

1 medium red onion, chopped
3 cloves of garlic, finely chopped
1 large tomato, diced
1 cup of cilantro, finely chopped
½ cup of olive oil, divided
1 teaspoon of oyster sauce
5 to 6 chicken thighs, cut 1-inch size, well trimmed off the fat
1 Adel sausage (Costco brand), thin sliced
1 teaspoon of basil
1 teaspoon of thyme
1 teaspoon of rosemary
¼ cup of finely chopped cheddar cheese
1 small yellow lemon, squeezed
pinch of salt and pepper to taste

PREPARATION

In a small bowl, mix oyster sauce, lemon juice, half of olive oil, basil, thyme, rosemary, salt, and pepper. Stir the preparation until all ingredients are well mixed and get a small paste.

In a large deep, nonstick, skillet, mix the onion, cilantro, garlic, tomato, and half of the oil. Cook over a low fire until mixture is soft.

Add the chicken and the sauce preparation to the mixture. Stir well until the chicken is well bathed in the preparation. Cook at low fire until the chicken is soft and tender.

Add the sliced sausage, cheese, and stir until all ingredients are well mixed.

In a separate pot, bring water to a boil, reduce the fire, and add the brown rice until it is cooked to your liking.

In a large dinner plate, serve a good portion of rice and top it with the chicken sauce, to your liking. Serve hot and accompanied with a semidry Riesling white wine or a good well-chilled Rose de Provence.

Enjoy!

CHICKEN WITH POTATOES

INGREDIENTS

6 to 8 chicken thighs
1 large tomato
½ red medium onion
3 to 4 medium potatoes
2 garlic cloves
1 teaspoon of sweet paprika
1 teaspoon of dry basil
1 teaspoon of dry oregano
1 teaspoon of oyster sauce
3 teaspoon of olive oil
½ cup of dry white wine
You could also use some parsley, finely chopped.

PREPARATION

Boil the potatoes to a soft center.

Clean and remove all the fat from the chicken thighs and pat dry.

Finely chop the onion and garlic.

In a medium-sized skillet and low fire, cook the olive oil, onion, garlic, tomato, and oyster sauce to a thick and caramelized sauce. Add the chicken, potatoes, and all the above spices. Cover and cook for 30 minutes until the chicken is tender. Add the white wine, and over a small fire, cook the chicken uncovered until all the wine has evaporated.

Serve with a glass of white wine and enjoy.

LEMON CHICKEN

For chicken lovers, this is a very simple and tasty recipe.

INGREDIENTS

¼ of good virgin olive oil
3 to 4 minced or crushed garlic (about 10 cloves)
1 medium yellow onion, chopped finely
1.3 cups of dry white wine
1 tablespoon of grated lemon zest (about 2 lemons)
2 tablespoons of freshly squeezed lemon juice
1 to 2 teaspoons of dry oregano
1 teaspoon of fresh thyme leaves, finely minced, or dry thyme
salt and pepper to your taste
4 to 6 pieces of chicken (breast, drums, or thighs, your choice)
1 lemon
1 handful of chopped cilantro

PREPARATION

Preheat oven at 400 °F.

In a saucepan, over medium-high heat, warm the olive oil, add the onion to be caramelized, then add the garlic for another 1 or 2 minutes without making it too dark.

Turn the heat to a very low and add the white wine, lemon zest, lemon juice, oregano, thyme, salt, and pepper. Cook for about 3 to 5 minutes.

Pour the whole mixture into a baking dish, large enough to accommodate your chicken.

Brush the chicken with olive oil, sprinkle with salt and pepper, and place it on top of the mixture in the baking dish.

Cut the lemon in 8 wedges and tuck it in between the chicken.

Bake the chicken for 30 to 40 minutes until the chicken is tender, then put the baking dish under the broiler to brown the chicken for a few minutes. Make sure you watch the chicken to not burn it.

Remove the baking dish from the oven; cover it tightly with aluminum foil paper to rest for about 10 to 15 minutes.

Serve hot with the pan's juice and sprinkle with cilantro and a glass of white wine.

You can add baked potatoes as a vegetable.

Enjoy!

CHICKEN DRUMS WITH TOMATOES

It is an easy recipe to make using only chicken drums, tomatoes, sundry tomatoes, garlic, and caramelized onion.

INGREDIENTS

8 or 10 chicken drums (legs) without skin
3 to 4 finely chopped garlic cloves
1 large yellow onion, finely chopped
1 large bay leaf
1 cup of sun-dried tomatoes
2 to 3 large wine tomatoes
1 tablespoon of dry oregano
1 tablespoon of dry or fresh basil
1 tablespoon of dry or fresh thyme
salt and black ground pepper to taste
1 cup of dry white wine
4 or 6 mushrooms, well washed and cut in small pieces

PREPARATION

Put the wine tomatoes into a bowl with boiling water for 1 minute, then peel the tomatoes, then cut in small pieces.

In a large skillet, caramelize the onion over a medium-high heat for 4 to 5 minutes or until the onion becomes translucent.

Add the garlic, bay leaf, oregano, thyme, basil, the sun-dried tomatoes, peeled tomatoes, cup of wine, salt, and pepper and let it cook in a very low heat for 10 minutes by stirring it quite often to make sure that the sauce is very well mixed.

Put all the chicken drums on top of the sauce, add the mushrooms, cover the skillet, and let it simmer for another 15 minutes until the chicken drums are tender. Make sure to cover the drums with the sauce as it is simmering.

Serve hot with ample sauce accompanied with a vegetable of your choice. I suggest steamed asparagus and a good glass of white wine.

Enjoy!

CHICKEN DRUMS STEW WITH POTATOES

During wintertime, when it is cold and rainy, it is always comfortable to have a good hearty hot dinner with a good glass of red wine. You could also have this dish any time without having to wait for cold weather.

INGREDIENTS

5 to 6 chicken thighs with the skin
5 to 8 round small white potatoes
1 cup of sun-dried tomatoes
3 to 4 garlic cloves, very finely minced
1 large red onion, chopped into very small pieces
salt and black pepper to taste
1 can diced tomatoes
2 to 3 wine tomatoes
1 teaspoon dry basil
1 teaspoon dry oregano
1 teaspoon dry thyme
$1/_3$ teaspoon turmeric
1 cup cilantro, chopped finely
1 cup red wine
2 tablespoons good virgin olive oil, separated

PREPARATION

In a large skillet, on a low heat, use 1 tablespoon of olive oil and caramelize the red onion until it is soft and translucent. Add the crushed garlic, the can of diced tomatoes, and let it simmer.

In a separate bowl filled with boiling water, put the wine tomatoes for a minute to remove the skin easily. Cut the tomatoes in small pieces and add to the skillet.

Let it cook for about 5 minutes, stirring it well.

To the skillet, add the rest of olive oil, basil, oregano, thyme, turmeric, salt, pepper, sun-dried tomatoes, cilantro, potatoes, red wine, and cook over medium-high heat for 2 minutes.

Spread the chicken thighs around the skillet and reduce the heat to low.

About 5 to 8 minutes, scoop the sauce with a large spoon and cover the chicken with the sauce until it is well covered.

Cover the skillet and cook the stew for another 20 minutes until the chicken is tender. Remove the cover and put the skillet into the oven and broil the chicken for about 2 minutes until the skin is well browned.

It is to be served hot and with the thighs covered with the sauce.

The whole dinner was accompanied with a glass of the same red wine.

Enjoy!

GABRIEL'S CHICKEN THIGHS

If you like chicken thighs, you can prepare this dish very delicious and quick.

INGREDIENTS.

6 or 8 boneless chicken thighs without skin, cut into cubes of 1 inch
2 tablespoons of good extra-virgin olive oil
3 to 4 garlic cloves, finely chopped
1 large red onion, finely minced
1 cup sun-dried tomatoes
3 large wine tomatoes
1 can of diced tomatoes
2 celery sticks, cut in 2-inch pieces
1 large bay leaf
1 teaspoon dry basil
1 teaspoon dry thyme
1 teaspoon dry oregano
1 cup of finely chopped Italian parsley
1 cup of red wine
½ cup of freshly squeezed lemon juice
salt and pepper to taste
4 to 6 medium-sized mushrooms, well washed and cut in small pieces

PREPARATION

In a large bowl full of boiling water, put the wine tomatoes for 2 minutes, peel, and cut into small pieces. Put aside.

In a large skillet over a medium heat, pour the olive oil. Add the chopped red onion and caramelize it until it is translucent. Add the garlic, the cut tomatoes, the diced tomatoes, and the sun-dried tomatoes. Cook for about 5 minutes.

Add oregano, basil, thyme, bay leaf, and celery for two or three minutes.

Add the red wine and stir over low heat. Add the chicken; stir well to mix with the sauce.

Once the chicken is tender, add the mushrooms, cover the skillet, and cook for another 5 minutes.

Serve the chicken hot with plenty of sauce and a glass of red wine.

This dish could be accompanied with potatoes, which could be added to the stew at the onset of the cooking, i.e., just after you put the tomatoes.

Enjoy!

ROULEAU POULET EN SAUCISSON BY MOTHER

(Rolled Chicken Sausage)

This is one of my mother's recipes that she used to make as an appetizer and serve as an aperitif when guests will come to visit her.

It is a bit complicated, but I will try to recreate it.

INGREDIENTS

1 whole fresh chicken
½ pound of ground veal
salt and white pepper
¼ teaspoon of saffron
1 pinch of cayenne
2 eggs
½ tablespoon of olive oil

PREPARATION

Remove the chicken skin by making a slit on the belly. Pull the skin from one side, then the other side, without tearing the skin into pieces. Remove the whole entire skin from the chicken.

Once the skin is removed, put it aside to be used for staffing the sausage.

Remove the chicken meat as much as possible and cut it as fine as possible in very small pieces. For the chicken meat that you cannot remove, boil the skeleton in water, which makes it easier to remove the rest of the chicken meat. Add it to the previous chicken pieces. Add the ground veal, season with some salt, white pepper, saffron, a pinch of cayenne, olive oil, and 2 eggs. Mix well and set aside.

Over a piece of transparent wet veil, lay flat the chicken skin, then spread the mixture well packed to cover the whole skin. Roll the veil, the skin, and the mixture from one side to the other, making like a sausage, then fold over the two ends like a package.

Sew the four sides to close the sausage.

Put the sausage into boiling water in a pan by turning it over quite often for the sausage to cook evenly. Once cooked, keep it refrigerated until the day you want to serve it without any water. Dry.

When you are ready to serve it, put the whole sausage into a baking pan, add some olive oil to the pan, and cook it in the oven at 325° for 5 to 10 minutes to make it ready to be eaten with a good glass of white wine. *Enjoy!*

CHICKEN DRUMS WITH WHITE POTATOES

This is a meal I often make because it is tasty and easy to make.

INGREDIENTS

4 to 6 chicken drums

4 to 6 white potatoes, sliced in ¼ of inch

1 teaspoon ground basil

1 teaspoon ground oregano

1 teaspoon ground thyme

salt and pepper to taste

2 to 4 garlic gloves, very finely minced

1 tablespoon olive oil

½ large red or yellow onion chopped in small pieces

1 cup white wine

1 cup parsley, finely chopped

PREPARATION

In a large skillet, put the olive oil and caramelize the onion until they are translucent. Add the garlic, salt, pepper, basil, oregano, thyme, parsley, and wine. Cook under a very low heat for about 10 minutes. Set aside.

In a nonstick baking dish, lay in one layer the potatoes and lay on top the chicken drums, then pour the mixture on top of the drum and put in the oven previously heated at 350 °F for 40 minutes.

After 40 minutes, change the oven setting to broil on high and change the baking dish on top to the broil oven tray. Leave the chicken for 10 minutes until you get a brownish color.

To be served hot with the same wine that you cooked with.

Enjoy!

CHICKEN DRUMS WITH VEGETABLES À LA GABRIEL

When you feel like eating a roasted chicken and you do not want to make the whole chicken, some roasted drums will do the trick, accompanied with steamed vegetables.

INGREDIENTS

3 to 6 chicken drums
½ pound asparagus
½ pound green beans
2 garlic, finely minced
1 cup brown sugar
2 to 3 cups apple cider vinegar
½ white onion, very finely chopped
salt and pepper to taste
½ cup ketchup
1 tablespoon Dijon mustard

PREPARATION

Preheat the oven at 350 °F.

In a separate bowl, put together garlic, brown sugar, apple vinegar, white onion, salt, pepper, ketchup, and Dijon mustard. Stir well until you get a thicker paste.

Pour the whole sauce into a mixer and blend the whole paste until liquefied.

In a separate baking dish sprayed with nonstick cooking PAM, lay the drums and paste them with the sauce until well covered. Put in the oven for 40 minutes, making sure that you rotate them every 20 minutes. Turn the oven off and set it up on high broil. Set your baking dish for 5 minutes, rotating them several times to make sure they are well exposed to the broiling heat. When satisfied with the look of the drums, well browned, set aside to cool off.

In a steamer with boiling water, steam your vegetables—asparagus and green beans—until tender when poked with a fork.

Serve the chicken drums and the vegetables together with a great glass of rosé or white zinfandel.

Enjoy!

MOROCCAN CHICKEN WITH OLIVES

A bit spicy but a very good delicacy. If you like chicken, you will love this Moroccan spicy recipe.

6 or 7 chicken thighs, cleaned and boneless
1 cup of Kalamata olives, washed and without pits
1 lemon, thin round slices
1 tablespoon all seasoning herbs
½ cup virgin olive oil, divided
2 to 3 cloves of garlic, finely minced
1 tablespoon ground cumin
1 tablespoon ground paprika
1 tablespoon ground turmeric
1 teaspoon cayenne pepper (optional)
1 medium sweet onion, sliced lengthwise
1 cup yellow rice mix

PREPARATION

Preheat the oven at 450 °F.

Line up a baking sheet with foil paper. In a separate bowl, toss together onions, all seasoning herbs, olives, lemon round slices, some olive oil, and pour over the baking sheet.

In a different bowl, mix together olive oil, all seasoning herbs, cumin, turmeric, paprika, garlic, and cayenne (optional). With this mixture, rub the chicken thighs very thoroughly all over and arrange the chicken over the baking sheet on top of the vegetables.

Put in the oven for 30 to 40 minutes until the chicken is tender or a thermometer reading of 180 °F. Remove the chicken from the oven and let it rest.

In a medium saucepan over a medium-high heat, bring 2 cups of water to a boil. Add the rice and a tablespoon of olive oil to boil for a minute, cover the saucepan, and reduce the heat to a low heat. Let it simmer until the water has evaporated and the rice is tender, about 30 minutes.

Serve the chicken on top of the vegetables; arrange the olive and the rice along the thighs. You can garnish the plate with some lemon slices also.

Enjoy with a glass of dry white wine.

CHICKEN WITH CARROT AND CELERY

On any weekday you feel like eating something tasty without too much work, try this chicken recipe, which can be done with any part of the chicken. It happens that I like to make it with chicken thighs.

INGREDIENTS

4 to 6 boneless and skinless chicken thighs, washed and pat dry
2 to 3 cloves of garlic
3 chive sticks, finely chopped
½ cup of parsley, finely chopped
3 medium carrots, peeled, washed, and round-sliced
5 celery sticks, washed and cut to 2-inch pieces
1 large or 2 small bay leaves
1 can diced tomatoes
1 cup sun-dried tomatoes
1 teaspoon basil
1 teaspoon paprika
½ teaspoon turmeric
salt and pepper to taste
½ cup olive oil

PREPARATION

In a large and deep skillet, pour 3 tablespoons olive oil, carrots, garlic, and the celery over a medium heat to sauté the vegetables. Once the carrots and the celery are tender, add the can of diced tomatoes, bay leaves, salt, pepper, basil, paprika, turmeric, the remaining olive oil, and the sun-dried tomatoes. Cook over a small heat while stirring to get a good mixture for 10 minutes.

Add the diced chicken, the chives, and the parsley and let it simmer for another 10 to 15 minutes until the chicken is very tender.

You can serve this dish with a side of salad of cucumber and diced tomatoes.

Enjoy with a good glass of white zinfandel.

CHICKEN BREAST RAGOUT

Today, I went to the market and found out that there was a special on chicken breast. I bought a pack of 4 breasts that I filleted and prepared like a ragout.

INGREDIENTS

4 large breasts of chicken, filleted, washed, and trimmed of the fat
3 cloves garlic, finely minced
1 teaspoon basil
1 teaspoon oregano
1 teaspoon sweet paprika
salt and pepper to taste
½ yellow onion, finely chopped
1.2 cups sun-dried tomato
1 wine tomato, peeled and cut into
   small cubes
2 bay leaves
½ cup fresh parsley, finely chopped
1 can diced tomatoes
½ cup olive oil, separated
1 cup of white wine

PREPARATION

In a large skillet over medium heat, pour ¼ olive oil, onion, and garlic. Cook until the onion is translucent. Reduce the heat to low. Add the diced tomatoes, the cubed tomatoes, bay leaves, basil, oregano, paprika salt, and pepper.. Keep stirring while cooking. To this mixture, add the sun-dried tomatoes and pour the wine. Let it simmer for 2 to 3 minutes and lay the fillets on top of the sauce and cook over a low heat. With a large spoon, keep putting the sauce over the chicken several times to keep it moist until tender.

Serve hot with a glass of white wine.

Enjoy!

TURKEY BALLS WITH CARROTS AND CELERY

When you feel like eating a good meal, this recipe is one of my favorite, especially the fact that I am using some spices that will make this dish absolutely delicious.

INGREDIENTS

2 pounds ground turkey
1 cup chives, chopped finely and separated
2 to 3 cloves garlic, finely chopped and separated
1 teaspoon turmeric
1 teaspoon ground basil
1 teaspoon ground thyme
1 teaspoon sweet paprika
salt and pepper to taste
1 cup sun-dried tomatoes
1 cup olive oil, separated
1 egg
1 cup parsley, finely chopped
1 large carrot, peeled and cut into 1-inch
    slices and cut in quarters
1 celery stalk, cut into 1-inch slices
1 cup of white zinfandel wine
2 bay leaves

PREPARATION

In a separate bowl, mix the ground turkey, egg, basil, turmeric, basil, parsley, garlic, paprika, olive oil, and chopped chive. Mix very well until all ingredients are all mixed.

In a large skillet, bring to a boil olive oil, chopped chives, garlic, salt, and pepper. Reduce the heat to medium and add celery, carrots, sun-dried tomatoes, bay leaves, and the wine. Cook for 10 to 15 minutes.

From the mixture previously made, make 2-inch turkey balls and add them to the skillet. Cook for 10 to 15 minutes by spraying the sauce over the turkey ball for the ball to absorb the sauce very well.

When the carrots and celery are tender to the fork, the turkey balls are to be served.

Enjoy with a glass of the same wine you cooked the turkey balls.

ROASTED CHICKEN THIGHS WITH POTATOES

This is one of the recipes that I enjoy eating because it is easy to prepare and so delicious to your palate, and of course, perfect with a good red wine.

INGREDIENTS

4 large chicken thighs, washed, trimmed from extra fat, and pat dry
2 large cloves of garlic, crushed
1 tablespoon of Dijon mustard
½ lemon juice
½ cup olive oil
2 sprouts of fresh basil, separated
2 sprouts of fresh rosemary
2 large baking potatoes, cut in ¼-inch slices
pinch of black pepper
2 large bay leaves

PREPARATION

In a large baking dish, spray nonstick PAM. Lay in rolls and cut potatoes to cover the whole baking dish.

In a separate bowl, add garlic, olive oil, mustard, lemon juice, one sprout of finely chopped basil, and pepper. With a spoon, stir well until you get a thick mixture.

With a brush, paint the potatoes with the mixture on both sides. Lay the chicken thighs on top of the potatoes and paint the chicken with the same mixture on both sides until well soaked in the sauce.

Lay on top of the chicken the 2 sprouts of rosemary and the 1 sprout left of basil and add the 2 bay leaves.

Preheat the oven at 350°.

Cover the baking dish with foil paper and bake for 40 minutes or until the potatoes are tender when tested with a fork.

Serve hot and *enjoy* with a good glass of red wine. You can also use a nice chilled white wine of your choice.

RATATOUILLE WITH TOMATO SAUCE AND CHICKEN

If you like eggplant, zucchini, and celery, here is a good dish that is easy to make and delicious to enjoy.

INGREDIENTS

3 to 5 chicken drums or any dark chicken meat of your preference
2 large cloves of garlic, very finely chopped
1 large zucchini, cut in cubes
1 large eggplant, cut in 1-inch cubes
2 stalks of celery, cut in 1-inch pieces
1 large or 2 small bay leaves
1 pinch of ground pepper
1 pinch of regular salt
1 teaspoon of ground basil
1 teaspoon of ground oregano
1 teaspoon of sweet paprika
1 teaspoon of turmeric or saffron, if
   you have any
1 cup of sun-dried tomatoes
½ red onion, finely chopped
½ cup of olive oil
1 can of tomato sauce

PREPARATION

In a large skillet, mix the olive oil, the onion, and the garlic. Cook over medium heat until the onion is transparent and soft.

Add the basil, the paprika, the oregano, the turmeric, the bay leaves, the ground pepper, the salt, and the sun-dried tomatoes. Cook at a low heat for 5 to 10 minutes. Add the eggplant, the zucchini, and the celery and keep stirring until well mixed. Add the tomato sauce and stir very well to make sure that all the mixture is well covered. Cook for 5 minutes with a very low heat and add the chicken drums or any chicken of your choice. During the cooking with a very low heat, make sure that you keep pasting the chicken with the sauce.

If you like to cook with some wine, you can add a cup of white wine of your choice.

Serve hot and *enjoy* with the same wine.

CHICKEN RAGOUT

For chicken lovers, this chicken ragout recipe has not only all the vitamins possible but also the great taste to be eaten either as is or over a pasta of your choice. Of course, serve with a good glass of white zinfandel.

INGREDIENTS

    2 large chicken thighs, clean from all fat and cut into 2-inch pieces
    2 stalks of celery, cut into 1-inch pieces
    2 large zucchinis, cut into 1-inch pieces
    1 small eggplant, cut into 1-inch cubes
    2 to 4 cloves of garlic separated in two
    1 pinch of ground pepper
    1 pinch of regular salt
    1 teaspoon of ground basil
    1 teaspoon of ground oregano
    1 teaspoon of sweet paprika
    1 teaspoon of turmeric or saffron, if you have any
    1 cup of sun-dried tomatoes

½ red onion, finely chopped
½ cup of olive oil, separated
1 can of tomato sauce
1 cup of white zinfandel

PREPARATION

In a separate skillet over medium heat, put all the following ingredients: ½ cup of olive oil, 2 large cloves of garlic, celery, zucchinis, eggplant, ground pepper, salt, basil, oregano, paprika, turmeric or saffron, sun-dried tomatoes, and tomato sauce. Cook and simmer for 15 to 20 minutes until celery is soft when tested with a fork. Put aside.

In a different skillet over medium heat, cook the red onion and 2 cloves of garlic until the onion is translucent. Add the chicken and the white zinfandel wine, and lower the heat until the chicken is cooked but still very tender by continuously watering the chicken with the wine sauce. To this skillet, add the above sauce and cook over a very low heat until you get a good thick sauce.

If you desire, you can serve it as is or added over some pasta of your choice that you have already prepared.

To be served hot with a good glass of white zinfandel.

Enjoy!

SAUTÉED CHICKEN WITH APPLE CIDER VINEGAR

The flavor of apple cider vinegar gives the chicken a totally different taste.

INGREDIENTS

2 to 3 chicken thighs, washed and cleaned from all fat, cut in pieces
1 tablespoon of basil
½ cup of apple cider vinegar
1 large clove of garlic, finely chopped
½ cup of chopped fresh parsley
salt and pepper to taste

PREPARATION

In a separate bowl, mix the chicken, parsley, garlic, salt, pepper, and apple cider vinegar.

Mix well until the chicken is well covered. Cover with saran wrap paper and refrigerate for 24 hours.

When ready to eat, in a skillet, pour the chicken and the sauce and cook under medium heat until chicken is tender and cooked.

Serve with any vegetable of your choice. I personally like it with brown rice.

Enjoy!

ROASTED CHICKEN THIGHS WITH MUSHROOMS AND POTATOES

INGREDIENTS

4 to 6 chicken thighs without skin, washed and pat dry
3 to 4 garlic cloves, crushed
dry basil
dry oregano
dry rosemary
½ cup of olive oil
2 bay leaves
½ lemon juice
salt and pepper to taste
1 to 2 cups of Veuve liquor champagne
6 red potatoes
8 large mushrooms

PREPARATION

In a separate bowl, mix garlic, lemon juice, salt, pepper, and olive oil.

Clean and pat dry the chicken thighs and put aside.

In a large baking dish, spray PAM and lay down the chicken thighs, keeping space in between.

Wash well the potatoes and cut them in cubes and spray in between the chicken thighs.

ROASTED CHICKEN THIGHS WITH POTATOES

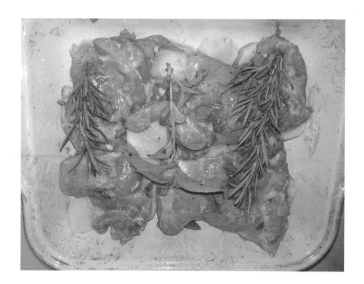

This dish can be made with any part of the chicken. I like it better with either thighs or drums.

INGREDIENTS

4 to 6 either chicken thighs or drums based to your liking
2 to 4 chopped cloves of garlic
½ cup of fresh finely chopped parsley
1 tablespoon of ground basil
1 tablespoon of ground oregano
½ cup of olive oil, separated
½ to ¼ cup of fresh squeezed lemon
salt and pepper to your liking
3 to 4 red or white potatoes, sliced in length

PREPARATION

Wash and pat dry the chicken and set aside.

In a separated bowl, pour the olive oil and add all the above ingredients. Mix well to blend all the ingredients until you get a well-thickened paste.

Add the chicken, and with a brush, make sure that all the chicken has been well covered with the paste. Cover and refrigerate for 2 to 3 hours.

In a separate baking dish covered with a nonstick spray (PAM), put all the cut potatoes like a layer and set aside.

When the chicken has been marinated for 2 or 3 hours, lay it on top of the potatoes, and with the same brush, make sure that you cover with the thickened paste all the potatoes. Pour the remaining sauce over the potatoes.

Preheat the oven at 350 °F and put the baking dish in the oven for 50 minutes.

When the chicken is ready, place the baking dish on the higher oven tray and put the oven on broil for 10 minutes.

The potatoes and the chicken will roast evenly.

Serve hot and accompany it with a glass of your favorite wine. I like merlot.

Enjoy!

ROASTED CHICKEN LEGS WITH POTATOES

If you like chicken legs and do not want to use the BBQ, here is a very simple and quick recipe that you can use a couple of hours before dinner.

INGREDIENTS

6 to 8 chicken legs without skin
2 to 3 garlic cloves, well crushed
½ cup squeezed lemon
1 tablespoon dry basil
1 tablespoon dry oregano
¼ tablespoon Dijon mustard
4 to 6 white potatoes, peeled and cut lengthwise
½ cup fresh parsley, finely chopped

PREPARATION

In a medium-sized bowl, mix garlic, basil, oregano, mustard, olive oil, lemon juice, and chopped parsley. Mix well until you get a thick paste. Set aside.

In a large baking dish sprayed with PAM, lay the potatoes and paste very well with the above-made sauce. Make sure that you use all the paste.

Put in the oven for 20 minutes at 350 °F.

In a separate bowl, marinate the chicken legs with olive oil, crushed garlic, well-chopped parsley, and lemon juice for 20 minutes.

When the potatoes are halfway cooked, lay the chicken legs on top of the potatoes and cook for another 30 minutes at 350 °F.

When the chicken legs are cooked, change the setting in your oven to hi-broil, and make sure that the baking dish is close to the broil in your oven.

After 10 minutes when the chicken legs are well roasted, remove from the oven and let it rest for 10 minutes.

Serve with potatoes and a chilled beer of your choice.

Enjoy!

MUSHROOMS WITH ROASTED CHICKEN AND POTATOES

As an appetizer, you cannot go wrong. Everybody loves mushrooms to enjoy with a glass of martini, vodka, scotch, tequila, or simply beer.

INGREDIENTS

4 to 6 full skinless thighs, marinated
1 or 2 pounds of brown mushrooms, sliced lengthwise about ⅛ of an inch
2 to 4 garlic cloves, finely crushed
1 pound of round red potatoes, cut in 4 quarters
½ cup of fresh parsley, chopped very finely
¼ teaspoon of sweet paprika
½ tablespoon ground basil
½ tablespoon ground oregano
½ cup lemon juice
¼ of tablespoon of ground sweet paprika
½ cup olive oil

½ cup cognac (good cognac of your choice)
salt and pepper to taste
2 tablespoons of oyster sauce (from Asian market, optional)
1 tablespoon of unsalted butter

PREPARATION

In a large bowl, mix olive oil, lemon juice, garlic, parsley, and oyster sauce. Add the chicken thighs and let marinate for 30 to 60 minutes aside. Do not refrigerate if you have to use it the same day.

In a separate bowl, mix olive oil, paprika, garlic, parsley, lemon juice, oyster sauce, cognac, basil, and oregano. Mix well until you get a thick sauce.

In a baking dish, spray with PAM and lay the potatoes that you will brush with the sauce until the potatoes are well covered and bake in the oven at 350 °F for 29 minutes.

Add to the baking dish the marinated chicken thighs by laying it over the potatoes. Put in the oven at 350 °F for 30 minutes until the chicken is tender to the fork.

In a large skillet, brown the mushrooms with salt, pepper, butter, garlic, parsley, and a tablespoon of cognac. Add to the chicken 10 minutes before serving.

To be served hot with a glass of white zinfandel.

Enjoy!

CHICKEN WITH POTATOES

This is a good lunch to serve when you are hungry, easy and simple to cook and, of course, delicious.

INGREDIENTS

4 to 6 chicken skinless drums, washed and pat dry
4 to 6 potatoes, washed, well peeled, and cut lengthwise
2 to 3 garlic cloves, finely chopped
1 cup fresh parsley, well chopped
1 tablespoon of ground basil
1 tablespoon of ground oregano
½ cup of lemon juice or apple vinegar, your choice
½ cup of olive oil
salt and pepper to taste

PREPARATION

Wash well and pat dry the chicken drums and set aside.

In a separate bowl, mix all together the ingredients very well and set aside.

In a baking dish sprayed with a nonstick spray, lay the potatoes, making sure to cover the whole baking dish. Lay on top of the potatoes the content of the bowl to cover the entire dish with the sauce.

Preheat the oven at 350 °F.

Put the baking dish in the oven for 30 minutes by moving the potatoes around.

Remove the potatoes and lay over the chicken drums.

Put in the oven for another 30 minutes until the chicken is cooked.

Serve hot and with a glass of wine to your liking.

Enjoy!

TURKEY BALLS IN TOMATO SAUCE

Turkey balls are always very good to have at home either frozen or fresh if you are hungry. You can always associate the turkey balls with any vegetable of your choice. The best that I like the most is with a good pasta and a glass of wine.

INGREDIENTS

1 pound of ground turkey
2 to 3 garlic cloves, well smashed and finely cut
1 cup of freshly chopped parsley
1 tablespoon of ground basil
1 tablespoon of ground oregano
1 teaspoon of ground cumin
1 egg
½ cup of olive oil, separated
1 can of diced tomatoes
salt and pepper to taste

PREPARATION

In a separate bowl, put the ground turkey and mix it with all the above ingredients until you get a good amalgam.

In a skillet, add to the rest of the olive oil the canned diced tomatoes, some crushed garlic, and some chopped parsley. Cook at medium heat until you get a good tomato sauce. Add the turkey balls and cook to a medium heat until the balls are ready to eat. To these turkey balls, you can add any vegetable or pasta of your choice. I usually add angel-hair pasta.

I enjoy this dish with a good white wine.

Enjoy!

MEAT

PASTA BOLOGNESE

If you decide to eat pasta, here is a simple and easy recipe that you can enjoy. This is a recipe that I learned and observed while I was traveling in Italy.

INGREDIENTS

1 medium white or red onion (vitamin C, vitamin B6, and potassium)

500 grams ground meat (preferably beef)

1 teaspoon of ground cumin (anticancer, helps to treat diarrhea, controls blood sugar, fights bacteria, has anti-inflammatory effects, lowers cholesterol, helps weight loss)

½ teaspoon of ground thyme (helps to fight a cold; source of copper, fiber, iron; and prevents itching)

½ teaspoon of ground oregano (antioxidants)

a cup of chopped coriander (cilantro) (dietary fiber, manganese, iron, magnesium, vitamin C and K, and protein)

3 cloves of fresh garlic crushed (manganese, vitamin B6, C, B1, potassium, iron; fights common cold, reduces blood pressure, improves cholesterol level to normal)

½ cup of olive oil

½ cup of water

1 egg

salt and Pepper to taste

1 large green pepper, well chopped

PREPARATION

Put the ground meat into a large bowl and mix all the above ingredients until you have a well-amalgamated meat. Cover and do not refrigerate. Just put aside.

In a medium pan, boil water; add a pinch of salt and a spoon of olive oil; put any pasta of your choice, preferably penne; and cook it until andante or to your taste.

In a large skillet, pour some olive oil and add chopped onion and green pepper. Cook the onion and pepper until the onion is soft and golden. Add the pasta, ½ cup of water where the pasta has been prepared, add some of the ground meat to your liking, and cook at a low fire for 10 minutes. Keep stirring the meat and the pasta together until it is well mixed.

Serve with a Cabernet Sauvignon red wine to your liking.

MEATBALLS WITH SWEET PEAS

INGREDIENTS

1 can of sweet peas to your choice
½ cup of olive oil
½ cup of water
1 large red or white onion, chopped
1 teaspoon of thyme
1 teaspoon of oregano
1 spoon of cumin
salt and pepper to your liking
500 grams meat of your choice, preferably beef
1 cup of chopped coriander (cilantro)
1 cup of white wine, preferably dry
1 egg
1 teaspoon of Montreal Steak seasoning
3 carrots, medium size, cut in small pieces

PREPARATION

In a large bowl, mix together the meat, half of the olive oil, water, thyme, cumin, oregano, Montreal Steak seasoning, egg, salt and pepper, and chopped coriander until you get a well-amalgamated meat.

Using the amalgamated meat, make meatballs about 1 inch in diameter. Place on a platter until you are ready to cook them.

In a large skillet, pour the other half of the olive oil, chopped onion, and carrots. Cook on low until the onion is soft and golden. Add the meatballs but leave a space between each meatball. Add water and the sweet peas.

Wait for about 5 minutes until the meatballs are cooked and add the white wine. Let simmer for about 10 minutes.

Serve warm with a glass of dry white wine.

MOROCCAN GRILLED LAMB CHOPS/STEAKS

INGREDIENTS

1 kilogram lamb chops
¼ cup chopped fresh mint
¼ cup chopped coriander (cilantro)
3 cloves garlic, crushed
2 tablespoons lemon juice
2 tablespoons olive oil

1 tablespoon cumin
1½ tablespoons paprika
salt and pepper to taste
½ teaspoon ginger
½ turmeric
1 tablespoon Montreal Steak (optional)

PREPARATION

Wash the chops or steaks and drain thoroughly. Dab with a paper towel for better results. In a large bowl, mix herbs, garlic, lemon juice, olive oil, and all the spices. Add the meat and mix well. Coat the meat evenly.

Cover the bowl and refrigerate overnight for best taste and results.

Preheat your grill, and before you start, spray cooking oil over the grill to prevent the meat from sticking.

Cook your meat according to the thickness of the cut and to your taste.

Serve with rice, potatoes or any grilled vegetable, and a red cabernet.

Enjoy!

GABRIEL'S SHREDDED BEEF

INGREDIENTS

2 pounds boneless beef chuck eye roast
kosher salt and pepper to taste
3 garlic cloves, minced
1 teaspoon vegetable oil or olive oil to taste
¼ teaspoon ground cumin
2 tablespoons of orange juice, freshly squeezed
1½ teaspoons grated lime zest
1 tablespoon lime juice
lime wedges for serving
1 onion, red or white, halved and sliced thin
2 tablespoons dry sherry
2 cups of water

PREPARATION

When trimming the meat, do not remove all visible fat. Some of it will be used as oil. Pull apart at the seams, trim, and cut into 1-inch cubes.

Bring the beef, 2 cups water, and 1¼ teaspoons salt to boil in a 12-inch nonstick skillet over medium-high heat. Reduce heat to low, cover, and gently simmer until the beef is very tender, about 1 hour and 45 minutes. (Check beep every 30 minutes, adding water so that the bottom third of beef is submerged.)

While beef simmers, combine garlic, oil, and cumin in a bowl. Combine orange juice and lime zest and lime juice in a second bowl.

Remove lid from skillet, increase heat to medium, and simmer until water and beef start to sizzle, 3 to 8 minutes. Using a slotted spoon, transfer beef to a rimmed baking sheet. Pour off and reserve fat from the skillet aside.

Rinse skillet clean and dry with a paper towel. Place a sheet of aluminum foil over beef, and using a meat pounder or heavy sauté pan, pound to flatten beef into ⅛-inch-thick pieces, discarding any large pieces of fat or connective tissue. (Some beef should separate into shred. Larger pieces that do not separate can be torn in half.)

Heat 1½ teaspoons reserved fat in an empty skillet over high heat. When fat begins to sizzle, add onion and ¼ teaspoon salt. Cook, stirring occasionally, until onion is golden brown and charred in spots, 5 to 8 minutes. Add sherry and ¼ cup water and cook until liquid evaporates, about 2 minutes. Transfer onion to bowl. Return skillet to high heat, add 1½ teaspoon reserved fat, and heat until it begins to sizzle. Add beef and cook, stirring frequently, until dark golden brown and crusty, 2 to 4 minutes.

Reduce heat to low and push beef to sides of skillet. Add garlic mixture to center and cook, stirring frequently, until fragrant and golden brown, about 30 seconds. Remove pan from heat, add orange juice mixture and onion, and toss to combine. Season with pepper to taste.

Serve immediately with lime wedges and A Good Year sauvignon blanc.

Enjoy!

LAMB AND EGGPLANT STEW WITH PITAS

This dish is one of my favorites, easy and simple to make and to enjoy.

INGREDIENTS

kosher salt

1 large eggplant (1½ pounds), sliced crosswise, ½-inch thick

¼ cup plus 2½ tablespoons vegetable oil

4 lamb shanks (about 1¼ pounds each)

freshly ground pepper

1 large white onion, chopped

½ cup pomegranate molasses (see note)

½ cup dried yellow split peas (3 ounces)

4 dried red chilies

2 teaspoons baharat spice blend (see note) or garam masala

2 teaspoons ground coriander

8 small pita breads, warmed and torn into large pieces

PREPARATION

In a bowl, dissolve 2 teaspoons of salt in 1 quart of water. Add the eggplant, cover with a small plate to keep the slices submerged, and let soak for 30 minutes.

In a large enameled cast-iron casserole pan, heat 2 tablespoons of the oil. Season the lamb with salt and pepper and cook over high heat, turning once, until well browned, about 5 minutes per side. Add the onion and cook over medium heat, stirring, until softened, 10 minutes. Add 3 quarts of water, the pomegranate molasses, split peas, dried chilies, *baharat*, and coriander and bring to a boil. Reduce the heat to low and simmer for 45 minutes, skimming and stirring a few times.

Drain the eggplant and pat dry. In a large nonstick skillet, heat 1½ tablespoons of the oil. Add one-third of the eggplant and cook over medium-high heat until browned, 3 minutes per side; transfer to paper towels to drain. Brown the remaining eggplant in the 3 tablespoons of oil. Add the eggplant to the lamb and simmer over low heat, stirring until the lamb is tender, 45 minutes.

Transfer the lamb to a rimmed baking sheet. Remove the meat from the bones and cut into 1-inch pieces. Boil the stew over high heat, skimming, until the liquid has reduced to 3 cups, about 40 minutes.

Return the lamb to the stew and season with salt and pepper. Divide the pita among 4 bowls. Ladle the stew on top and serve.

NOTES

Pomegranate molasses is basically reduced pomegranate juice.

Baharat is a complex spice blend typically containing cumin, coriander, and paprika. Both are available at Middle Eastern groceries stores.

GABRIEL'S KEFTA

INGREDIENTS

2 teaspoons smoked paprika
2 teaspoons ground cumin
1 teaspoon freshly ground black pepper
1 teaspoon ground coriander
½ teaspoon ground cinnamon
½ teaspoon ground nutmeg
¼ teaspoon ground cloves
¼ cup of olive pure (extra virgin)
¼ cup of water
1 egg

PREPARATION

Mix all ingredients in a center of 500 grams of ground meat until you get an even amalgam.

Make your keftas' patties—grilled, cooked, or barbequed—to your liking.

Enjoy with either beer if BBQ or wine if cooked.

MOROCCAN MEATBALLS IN TOMATO SAUCE

INGREDIENTS

1 15-ounce can of organic cut tomatoes
1 6-ounce can of tomato paste
2 large organic fresh tomatoes
1.5 pounds of lean ground beef
1 cup of mixed fresh finely cut parsley and cilantro
1 egg
½ cup of olive oil
1 teaspoon oregano
1 teaspoon basil
1 teaspoon ground red chili
1 teaspoon Montreal steak
2 teaspoons cumin
1 teaspoon sweet paprika (I use Hungarian paprika)
1 large bay leaf or 2 small ones
2 large finely cut garlic cloves

PREPARATION

In a large bowl, mix the ground meat with all the above spices (oregano, basil, ground red chili, Montreal steak, cumin, sweet paprika), including the egg, the olive oil, and the cup of mixed parsley/cilantro. Using your hand or a wooden spoon, mix very well until you achieve a good amalgam.

Prepare your meatballs, about one inch in size, and set aside.

In a nonstick skillet, pour the 2 cans of tomatoes with its own juice. Add the garlic and bay leaves and cook above a very low fire until you get a thick tomato sauce, about 30 minutes. Keep the skillet covered.

About 30 minutes before serving, add the meatballs to the tomato sauce, making sure that the meatballs are not touching one another, and let them cook over a low fire, skillet covered.

You can serve them over boiled potatoes, string beans, rice, or any pasta of your choice and of course a good cabernet or merlot of your liking.

MOM'S MEATBALLS

INGREDIENTS

2 pounds of lean ground meat
2 eggs
fresh coriander (cilantro)
1 teaspoon of nutmeg
1 teaspoon of pepper
1 yellow onion, chopped to very small pieces
1 tablespoon olive oil, separated
1 tablespoon bread crumbs
1 teaspoon curcumin
1 teaspoon saffron
1 cup frozen peas

PREPARATION

Use a regular bowl and mix all of the followings:

Precook the onion in a skillet until it becomes translucent. Add 2 pounds of meat. Put a large handful of fresh coriander, a spoon of nutmeg, pepper, onion, bread crumbs, and 2 eggs in the food processor. Beat everything and mix with meat.

Make the meatballs and put them in boiling water. They will drop a lot of foam.

Remove the meatballs and pass the sauce through a colander.

Return the sauce to the heat, add saffron or curcumin, return the meatballs to the sauce, add oil, and simmer over low heat.

As for the peas, I buy them frozen, and I put them in the microwave with a little water and oil for 8 minutes. I serve them with meatballs.

SLOW-COOKED LAMB SHANK

Lamb shanks are not very tender and require slow cooking for several hours to be tender and very tasty.

INGREDIENTS

1 sweet onion, finely cut
4 to 5 lamb shanks
1 teaspoon Worcestershire sauce or similar
1 teaspoon of kosher salt
ground black pepper to your taste
1 teaspoon olive oil
10 whole peeled garlic cloves (for stronger taste, mince the cloves)
10 whole mushrooms, washed and cleaned
½ cup of red wine
½ cup of beef broth (You can make your own. It is much tastier.)
1 can diced tomatoes
1 teaspoon dried oregano
1 teaspoon dried basil
4 sprigs fresh thyme or 1 teaspoon of dried thyme
1 teaspoon allspice
1 bay leaf
4 to 5 round white potatoes, sliced in ½-inch slices
1 to 2 carrots, cut in 1-inch-thick pieces
1 cup of cilantro, cut finely

HOW TO PREPARE THE LAMB SHANKS

Refrigerate the shanks overnight to reduce the fat by scraping off the congealed fat.

PREPARATION

Spread the onion at the bottom of the slow cooker.

Add the sliced potatoes and the carrots.

Rub shanks with Worcestershire sauce, then sprinkle with salt and pepper.

In a skillet, over medium-high fire, put the olive oil and brown the shanks all around. Transfer the shanks along with any browned pits to the slow cooker on top of the onion. Top the shanks with the garlic and mushrooms.

In a separate bowl, combine the wine, beef broth, diced tomatoes, oregano, basil, thyme, allspice, bay leaf, and cilantro. Mix well and pour the mixture over the shanks and the vegetable in the slow cooker.

Set the slow cooker on low and cook for 6 to 8 hours.

It is better to serve it the next day, after a night in the refrigerator. You can scoop or scrape the fat from the dish when it is still hard.

To be served with the same red wine used to cook.

Enjoy!

BEEF STEW

When it is freezing cold, a good hot and tasty beef stew is to be appreciated. Of course, a good glass of red wine or even a good beer could accompany the stew.

INGREDIENTS

2 pounds beef tri-tip, roast, or short ribs
½ cup of cooking oil (preferably olive oil, separated)
salt and black pepper
3 medium carrots, diced
1 large sweet onion, diced
3 medium celery sticks, diced
4 garlic cloves, minced
10 small mushrooms, sliced
2 tablespoons of unsalted butter
2 tablespoons of all-purpose flour
1 cup of red wine
1 cup of tomato sauce
2 tablespoons of Worcestershire sauce
4 cups of beef broth (You can make it yourself.)
2½ teaspoons of Italian herbs blend
1 teaspoon of smoked paprika or just regular paprika
½ tablespoon of granulated sugar
ground black pepper
3 to 4 cups of half baby potatoes
1 cup of fresh or frozen peas
2 tablespoons of fresh chopped Italian parsley

PREPARATION

Cut the beef into 1 to 1½-inch chunks. Preheat a large frying pan over medium-high heat and add a few tablespoons of olive oil. Once the pan is hot, add the cubed beef, season generously with salt, and fry for 7 to 10 minutes until well browned all over. Transfer the beef to a large slow cooker. Deglaze the frying pan with ½ cup of water and add the liquid to the slow cooker.

Into the same frying pan, add 1 tablespoon of olive oil and add the carrots, celery, and onion. Sauté the mixture over medium heat until the onions are translucent, about 4 to 5 minutes. Once the onion is tender, add the garlic and cook for one more minute. Transfer the mixture into the slow cooker.

Into the same frying pan, add the butter, allow it to melt, and add the mushrooms. Sauté the mushrooms for 4 to 5 minutes until well browned all over. Season the mushrooms with salt and pepper to taste, then add the flour. Toss the mushrooms in the flour so they are evenly coated and cook for another 1 minute. Transfer the mushrooms into the slow cooker.

To the slow cooker, add the red wine, tomato sauce, Worcestershire, beef broth, spices, and herbs. Season generously with black pepper and 1½ teaspoon of salt.

Cover the slow cooker and turn the setting on high heat to bring it to a boil. Once it is boiling, reduce the heat to low and let it simmer for 2 hours plus, until the beef is tender.

Once the beef is tender, add the potatoes and the frozen peas. Let it cook for another 20 minutes plus until the potatoes are tender.

Serve hot likes a soup with some chopped parsley.

Enjoy with a good glass of the same wine used for cooking.

SPAGHETTI WITH SAUSAGES

This delicious dish is done very quickly, if you are in a hurry or if you have nothing prepared for dinner.

INGREDIENTS

A handful of spaghetti or any pasta of your choice
¼ tablespoon olive oil
1 sausage of your choice, sliced
salt and pepper to taste
1 teaspoon ground oregano
1 teaspoon ground basil
1 cup parsley, finely chopped
1 to 2 garlic cloves, finely chopped

PREPARATION

In a separate boiling pan, cook your spaghetti until al dente.

In a skillet over medium heat, pour olive oil, garlic, oregano, basil, salt, and pepper and cook for 5 minutes, until garlic is starting to get brown. Add the sausage and sauté them for a few minutes.

Drain the pasta and add it to the skillet, stirring continuously until well mixed.

Enjoy with a glass of white wine.

IRISH LAMB STEW
À LA GABRIEL

When we were traveling in Ireland, we ate every day at the Irish pubs, where the food was cooked for local people. One day, we were lucky to be served with an Irish lamb stew, which was unbelievably delicious. Wanting to learn the recipe, I asked the cook, who was a woman, for the recipe, and to my astonishment, she gave it to me. I was as happy as anyone could be.

As soon as we got back home from our traveling, sure enough, I made the stew immediately, and of course, every time I made it, I changed the original recipe to my own taste.

INGREDIENTS

2 to 4 pounds of boneless shoulder, lamb steak, or leg of lamb cut into small pieces of 1 inch
2 to 3 tablespoons all-purpose flour
6 to 8 white potatoes, peeled cut into 1-inch pieces
1 yellow onion chopped into small pieces
2 to 4 carrots, peeled and cut into ½-inch pieces
2 sticks celery cut into ½-inch pieces
2 cups of beef broth (I make my own broth)
1 cup of red dry wine
¼ cup of tomato paste
salt and black pepper to taste
½ teaspoon of dry thyme
10 once of frozen peas, thawed
½ pound turnips (peeled and cut into 1-inch pieces)

PREPARATION

Coat the inside of the slow cooker with nonstick cooking spray. Toss lamb with flour and lay in the bottom of the slow cooker. Add potatoes, turnips, onions, carrots, and celery.

Combine broth with wine, tomato sauce, ½ teaspoon of salt, ¼ teaspoon of the pepper, and the thyme. Mix well and pour over the contents of the slow cooker.

Cover the slow cooker and cook on high for 6 hours or low for 8 hours. Stir in peas and remaining salt and pepper during the last 15 to 30 minutes of cooking time.

Serve with bread, a glass of wine, or even a dark beer. *Enjoy!*

DAFINA BY MY MOTHER

It is a traditional dish that all Moroccan Jews used to eat on Saturday for lunch.

The recipe varies from one city to another depending where your family was from. As far as I am concerned, I knew that my family came from the city of Rabat, which is still the capital of Morocco.

I have made this dish for my family several times, and my children are also making it for their own family, not for Saturday like the old time but any time they feel like eating it because it is a delicious traditional dish.

And here is the recipe for the dafina with rice that my mother used to make.

INGREDIENTS

4 to 6 white or red round potatoes, well peeled
whole entire clove of garlic, cleaned but not peeled
4 to 6 raw eggs
1 small yellow onion
2 tablespoons of brown rice (See preparation further down.)
salt and white pepper to taste
1 tablespoon of dry cumin
1 cup of olive oil, separated
1 or 2 pounds of chuck steak, depending for how many people
1 shank of beef with the bone
2 to 3 dates with no seed, cut into small pieces
2 cans of chickpeas, drained and dry
1 teaspoon of red paprika
1 tablespoon of sugar
1 teaspoon of honey

PREPARATION

Prepare the rice that will be used for the dafina.

In a frying pan, brown the onion and one clove of garlic, finely chopped with 4 tablespoons of olive oil over medium heat. Once the onion is translucent, add the brown rice and cover the rice with water. Bring to a boil, then reduce the heat until the water has evaporated completely. Pour the rice into cotton cloths and roll it like a sausage by sewing the two extremities well tight. Put aside.

In a slow cooker, pour the chickpeas, the potatoes by arranging them all around the pot, and add the eggs in the center of the potatoes. Place the pieces of meat, shank and chuck, on top of the eggs and potatoes and top with the roll of rice.

Once all the ingredients have been set in the slow cooker, pour on top the rest of the olive oil, the dates cut into small pieces, the sugar, and the honey.

Fill in the slow cooker with water to cover all the ingredients.

Set the setting in slowly, cover, and let it cook for 8 hours.

About 4 hours of cooking, check the water level to make sure it has not evaporated. If it did, add boiling water to cover all the ingredients.

To be served in different platters by arranging first the potatoes, then the eggs, then the meat, then the rice by removing it from the cloth. The chickpeas could be served in a sauce container like a soup or a sauce depending on how much you have left.

Some people like to add cayenne pepper to their plate. It is a matter of choice. Not mine.

It has always been a delicious dish.

Enjoy with a glass of red wine. Vodka has been also served with this dish.

RATATOUILLE BY MY MOTHER

I remember coming from school for lunch during wintertime when the weather was cold and rainy, my mother had already prepared the lunch with all the salads and the main course being eggplant with meat. Here is her recipe.

INGREDIENTS

2 eggplants washed and dried, diced 1 inch
1 can of diced tomatoes
2 garlic cloves, minced very finely
1 large red onion, finely chopped
1 cup of fresh parsley, finely chopped
1 teaspoon basil
1 teaspoon oregano
1 teaspoon saffron or turmeric
1 teaspoon of sweet paprika
salt and pepper to taste
1 pound of chuck steak meat, cut in strips ½-inch wide
2 large wine tomatoes, without skin, cut in small pieces
1 cup of sun-dried tomatoes
1 cup of virgin olive oil
1 cup of water

PREPARATION

In a large cooking pot, pour oil, onion, and garlic over medium heat. Cook until the onion is translucent. Add the meat and brown the meat for 2 minutes.

Add to the pot diced tomatoes, wine tomatoes, basil, oregano, paprika, salt, pepper, parsley, sun-dried tomatoes, saffron or turmeric, eggplant, and water. Cover and let it cook until the meat is tender. During the cooking, keep stirring to make sure that all the ingredients are being cooked evenly.

I remember it to be an excellent dish. Nowadays, I will accompany the dish with a good glass of red wine. *Enjoy!*

ROASTED PEPPER WITH GARLIC BY MY MOTHER

My mother used to prepare these roasted peppers as a salad only on Friday night dinner.

INGREDIENTS

6 to 8 poblano peppers, entire
2 to 4 garlic cloves, very well minced
2 tablespoons olive oil
1 cup cilantro
salt and pepper to taste
1 tablespoon lemon juice

PREPARATION

In an oven tray at 350 °F, put the peppers to roast for 30 minutes. It may take longer. Rotate the pepper regularly to roast them evenly. Once roasted, set aside to cool off.

In a large skillet, heat the oil over medium-high; add the garlic, the cilantro, the salt, and pepper. Mix well. Add the poblano pepper one next to the other and sauté them over low heat by rotating them regularly. Once they are fully cooked, place them in a large serving platter, lengthwise; pour the sauce (garlic, oil, cilantro, salt, and pepper) and the lemon juice over, and they are ready to be served.

It could also be used as an appetizer.

Enjoy!

RAGOUT OF LAMB WITH HERBS

If you like lamb, this is a good recipe to enjoy during wintertime with a good aroma floating in the house while the lamb is cooking.

INGREDIENTS

2 to 3 pounds of lamb roast, cut into 1-inch cubes
½ cup of virgin olive oil
1 large yellow onion, finely minced
2 to 3 cloves of garlic, finely minced
2 to 3 tablespoons of water
1 cup of tomato paste
3 tablespoons of flour
salt and pepper to taste
1 cup chicken broth
2 cups of Guinness beer or more if you desire
1 teaspoon basil
1 teaspoon oregano
1 teaspoon thyme
1 teaspoon paprika
4 to 6 white potatoes, peeled, washed, and round-sliced
1 cup of frozen peas
2 sticks of leeks, washed and cut in 1-inch pieces
2 sticks of celery, washed and cut in 1-inch pieces
½ cup of green cabbage, washed and shredded
2 carrot sticks, peeled, washed, and round-sliced
2 to 3 wine tomatoes cut into cubes

PREPARATION

Remove the fat from the lamb and cut it into 1-inch cubes. Season with salt and pepper and brown it in a skillet with 2 teaspoons of olive oil. Make sure the lamb is well browned all over. Remove from the skillet and set aside.

To the same skillet, add 2 tablespoons olive oil, onion, garlic, and 2 tablespoons of water. Cook for a few minutes until the onion is translucent. Add tomato paste and cook for a few more minutes. To this mixture, add the lamb already sprinkled with flour and cook while stirring to dissolve the flour. Add chicken broth, Guinness beer, water, all herbs, and mix well until all the ingredients are well blended.

In a slow cooker, lay down the carrots, leeks, celery, potatoes, tomatoes, peas, cabbage, and the remaining of olive oil. Pour over the contents of the skillet and add some water to cover all the contents in the slow cooker.

Set the slow cooker to a low setting and cook for a minimum of 8 hours.

Check every 2 to 3 hours to make sure that the contents are still covered with water. If the level of water is below the content, add some hot water to cover.

After a few hours of cooking, the whole house will have a tremendous good aroma, which will make you impatient to start eating.

Enjoy with a good glass of merlot.

SPAGHETTI MEATBALLS

If you feel like eating pasta, here is a recipe that takes time to cook but is delicious to eat and best enjoyed with a glass of merlot.

INGREDIENTS

1 or 2 pounds of ground meat (I use very lean beef and sometimes ground turkey.)

½ cup of well-chopped chives

2 to 3 cloves, finely chopped or smashed to your liking

2 to 3 zucchinis

1 tablespoon ground basil (If you have fresh basil, use it instead.)

1 tablespoon ground oregano

1 teaspoon ground paprika

1 tablespoon ground cumin

½ cup olive oil

1 cup sun-dried tomatoes

1 can of diced tomatoes

1 can of tomato sauce

1 egg

1 large bay leaf

any pasta of your liking (I use spaghetti.)

salt and pepper to taste

PREPARATION

In a separate bowl, prepare your ground meat by mixing egg, cumin, oregano, basil (if you use ground basil), salt and pepper, and smashed garlic. Mix well and make as many meatballs of 1- to 2-inch diameter and put aside.

In a large skillet over medium heat, sauté the chives, chopped garlic, fresh or ground basil, oregano, bay leaf, diced tomato, and paprika. Keep stirring to mix very well. Reduce the heat, add tomato sauce and the meatballs, and simmer for a good 20 minutes.

In a separate pot, bring some water to boil, add a pinch of salt and a teaspoon of olive oil, and add the pasta. Reduce the heat to medium heat and cook the pasta to become al dente.

Serve the pasta and the meatballs with as much tomato sauce as you like. A glass of Chianti or merlot will do the trick.

Enjoy!

ROASTED LEG OF LAMB

For the readers who love lamb, here is a great and tasty recipe.

INGREDIENTS

    3 to 4 pounds boneless leg of lamb
    10 small cloves of garlic
    10 sprouts of fresh rosemary
    ¼ cup olive oil
    3 tablespoons Dijon mustard
    5 to 6 small round potatoes, peeled and cut in quarters
    1 flat can of anchovies
    1 cup red wine
    4 to 5 medium brown mushrooms
    1 teaspoon of regular flour

PREPARATION

Preheat the oven at 350 °F.

Prepare the leg of lamb by washing it with cold water. Dry and set aside.

In a large baking porcelain dish, spray with nonstick PAM all around the baking dish and place the dry leg of the lamb.

With a small sharp knife, on the flat side of the lamb, make a small hole and insert a small clove of garlic, a rosemary sprout, and half of an anchovy all together in the hole. Do it all over the side of the lamb like soldiers, one next and behind each other.

In a different bowl, mix olive oil, crushed garlic, and mustard.

Once one entire side of the leg of lamb is covered with garlic, rosemary, and anchovy, paste all over the lamb the mixture.

Lay the potatoes in the baking dish and lay over the lamb.

Cover with foil paper tightly and put in the oven. Set the cooking time at 20 minutes per pound.

The lamb is ready when tender with a fork. Turn the heat off and set aside the lamb to cool off.

In a separate small pot, pour the juice from the lamb baking dish, wine, mushrooms, and the flour. Bring to a boil, then reduce the heat to medium and keep stirring the sauce until you get a good thick gravy.

When you want to serve the lamb, cut slices against the grain.

Serve the lamb and the potatoes apart, add the gravy, and *enjoy* with a glass of merlot or your favorite red wine.

STUFFED ZUCCHINI

Zucchini are a good source of health-protecting antioxidants and phytonutrients, including vitamin C, beta-carotene, manganese, zeaxanthin, and lutein.

Lutein is to be taken in consideration as being a preventive for macular degeneration.

Therefore, this recipe is easy to make and delicious to eat.

INGREDIENTS

1 pound of any ground meat of your choice (I make it with ground turkey)
1 tablespoon of ground basil
1 tablespoon of ground thyme
1 tablespoon of ground cumin
1 teaspoon of paprika
1 egg
1 cup of finely chopped fresh parsley
salt and pepper to taste
3 large cloves of garlic, finely crushed and separated
2 large zucchinis, cut in length
1 can diced tomatoes
2 bay leaves
½ cup olive oil, separated

PREPARATION

In a separate bowl, put the ground meat and add egg, cumin, basil, thyme, 2 crushed garlic, salt, pepper, parsley, and olive oil. Mix very well until all the ingredients are well bound together. Set aside.

In a large skillet, sauté the garlic, parsley, bay leaves, can of tomatoes, paprika, zucchinis, and olive oil. Stir well and cook under medium heat until zucchinis are not too tender to the fork. Set aside to cool off.

When the zucchini cools down and with the help of a teaspoon, remove the center of the zucchinis and make it like a tranche. Stuff in the zucchinis with the prepared ground meat well packed and set in a baking dish. Cook in the oven for 20 minutes.

You can use this recipe for the vegetarian people by stuffing the zucchini with some rice mixed with the center of the zucchini and mushroom.

To be enjoyed with a glass of beer.

PORK SIRLOIN WITH POTATOES

This is a wonderful dinner when you want to entertain some of your dearest friends. Of course, it must be accompanied with the proper wine, such as white zinfandel.

INGREDIENTS

1 large 3- to 4-pound pork sirloin, sliced in ½ inch. Remove all fat.
3 to 4 large white potatoes, peeled and cut lengthwise
2 to 3 garlic cloves, finely chopped
olive oil
1 tablespoon Dijon mustard
1 cup of parsley and cilantro, finely chopped
1 tablespoon dry basil
1 tablespoon dry oregano
1 sprout of rosemary to be removed before serving
1 squeezed lemon juice to be used for baking the potatoes
1 cup of white zinfandel wine to accompany the dinner
salt and pepper to taste

PREPARATION

In a large baking glass dish, spray with nonstick PAM, lay the potatoes already cut lengthwise, and paste the potatoes with the prepared sauce.

In a separate bowl, mix the olive oil, crushed garlic, basil, oregano, lemon juice, Dijon mustard, salt, and pepper. Mix very well until you get a thick paste that you will apply to the potatoes with a brush until all potatoes are well coated.

Put the baking dish in the oven at 350° for 20 minutes. Make sure that you mix the potatoes as it is baking.

Add the sliced meat and the wine over the potatoes and continue baking until the meat is nicely cooked.

Depending on your taste, the pork sirloin should be cooked medium rare to medium, never well-done.

To be served with either rice, steamed asparagus, or any other green vegetable.

Enjoy with a chilly glass of white zinfandel.

TAGINE OF LAMB WITH DRIED PRUNES AND ALMONDS

For the people who like lamb, here is an easy recipe to enjoy and savor the taste of lamb accompanied with prunes and almonds.

INGREDIENTS

3 to 4 pounds of fat-free lamb roast, cut in cubes
1 large onion, chopped very finely
¾ cup of olive oil
1 tablespoon ginger
1 tablespoon ground cinnamon
½ cup of coriander (cilantro)
salt and pepper to taste
¼ teaspoon of saffron
1 to 2 garlic cloves, finely crushed
1 tea bag to be used to soak the dried prunes
½ pound of dried prunes
½ pound of almond, previously soaked and peeled
1 tablespoon of honey
1 tablespoon of unsalted butter

PREPARATION

Soak the dried prunes in hot tea until soft. Remove and set aside.

In a large skillet, caramelize the onion in olive oil until soft and golden color, remove, set aside, and replace by adding the lamb.

When the lamb is getting to a golden color, remove it and put it in a large baking dish. Add onion, salt, pepper, garlic, cinnamon, ginger, saffron, and coriander (cilantro).

Add water to cover the meat, cover, and cook for at least one hour at low fire.

When the meat is tender to the fork, add the prunes after being drained for another 20 to 30 minutes, still covered.

In a different skillet, brown the almonds in the butter until well goldened. Remove and add it to the meat with the honey.

Cook for another 5 to 10 more minutes, uncovered, until the lamb is very soft.

Serve with couscous.

Enjoy with a good glass of merlot.

STEAK "ARRACHERA" MARINATED

When I was visiting Mexico during the summer of 2021, I had lunch in a well-known Mexican restaurant where I was able to order a steak called arrachera.

To my surprise, the meat was very tender and extremely tasty.

I asked the waiter to give me the recipe that I have been making at home ever since. The picture is the one from the restaurant.

INGREDIENTS

- 1 piece of steak, such as flank or skirt steak, that you can find at any market or even at your butcher
- ½ cup of apple vinegar
- salt and pepper to taste
- 1 clove of garlic, well chopped
- ¼ cup of fresh parsley, chopped very finely
- 1 teaspoon of paprika
- ½ cup of Worcestershire sauce

PREPARATION

Combine all the above ingredients in a big bowl. Add the steak and brush it with a brush all over and set aside in the refrigerator to marinate for 2 hours.

Before putting the steak on a grill, make sure that the steak is out of the refrigerator for at least 30 minutes

When grilling the meat, keep brushing it until cooked to your desired cooking.

Serve with any kind of green vegetables and enjoy!

LAMB SIRLOIN WITH PRUNES AND ALMONDS

For a good entertainment dinner, this lamb recipe could do it quite nicely. Of course, it is accompanied with a good Malbec or merlot as a red wine. It may take several steps to cook this wonderful meal, but the end result is worth it.

INGREDIENTS

2 to 3 pounds lamb sirloin, cut in ½-inch slice
2 cups of prunes
1 cup of almonds
1 large white onion, chopped very finely
4 cloves of garlic, crushed or finely chopped
1 tablespoon cinnamon
1 tablespoon ginger
½ tablespoon saffron
¼ cup of coriander seeds
1 tablespoon honey
1 to 2 tea bags (any tea bag)
2 tablespoons unsalted butter
½ cup olive oil

PREPARATION

In a separate bowl, soak the prunes in a hot tea for 10 to 15 minutes.

In a skillet, use olive oil to caramelize the onion until well translucent and golden.

Remove the onion and put aside in a bowl to rest.

Use the same skillet to start golden the lamb until all faces are gold in color.

Remove the lamb and transfer it to a large baking dish already sprayed with PAM.

Lay the lamb like soldiers to cover the baking dish and cover the lamb with the caramelized onion. Make sure that all pieces of lamb are covered with the onion.

On top of the caramelized onion, lay the crushed garlic, the cinnamon, the ginger, the saffron, and the coriander seeds.

Preheat the oven at 350 °F.

Add water to cover the meat, put a lid on, and put in the oven for 90 minutes.

While the lamb is baking, put all the prunes and let it drain from all the tea.

Once the lamb is tender to the fork, add the drained prunes over the lamb and put it back in the oven with the lid on for another 30 minutes.

In a separate skillet, add butter, honey, and almonds until well browned and crispy.

Add to the meat by making sure it is well sprayed to cover the whole dish.

Put back in the oven uncovered for another 10 minutes.

Serve with couscous that you can prepare according to the package.

Yum, it is delicious with a good glass of red wine.

Enjoy!

LAMB CHOPS WITH POTATOES

Here is a dish for some people who love lamb, very easy to prepare and cook.

INGREDIENTS

4 to 6 red potatoes, peeled and sliced lengthwise
4 to 6 lamb chops, cleaned and pat dry
2 to 4 cloves of garlic, finely chopped
½ cup of fresh parsley, finely chopped
salt and pepper to taste
1 tablespoon of ground basil
1 tablespoon of ground oregano
1 tablespoon of ground cumin
½ cup of olive oil

PREPARATION

In a baking dish sprayed with a nonstick spray, lay the potatoes like soldiers and set aside.

In a separate bowl, mix all the above ingredients to make a thick sauce and marinate the lamb chops for 30 minutes.

Lay the lamb chops on top of the potatoes, and with a brush, apply the sauce to the potatoes until well covered with the sauce.

Preheat the oven at 350 °F.

Bake the whole dish for 30 minutes. When the lamb chops are well cooked, remove the baking dish and place it higher in the oven and broil it for 10 minutes.

Serve hot with a glass of wine.

Enjoy!

POTATOES WITH SAUSAGES

This is a dish that is very easy and simple to make, also very inexpensive and delicious.

INGREDIENTS

3 to 6 potatoes, washed and cut in length

2 to 4 garlic cloves, finely chopped

2 to 4 sausages, already cooked and cut in ½-inch slice

1 tablespoon of ground basil

1 tablespoon of ground oregano

½ tablespoon of ground cumin

1 cup for chopped fresh parsley

½ teaspoon of sweet paprika

1 cup of chopped chives (optional)

½ cup lemon juice or apple vinegar

½ cup olive oil

salt and pepper to taste

PREPARATION

In a baking dish sprayed with nonstick spray, lay the potatoes to cover the dish.

In a separate bowl, mix all together the above ingredients, and with a brush, lay the sauce over the potatoes to cover it all.

Preheat the oven at 350 °F.

Put the baking dish in the oven for 30 minutes by making sure to mix all the potatoes while cooking.

Remove the potatoes and lay over the sausages to cover the potatoes. Put in the oven for another 10 minutes.

Remove for the oven and serve hot with either some cold beer to your choice or a good well-chilled Pinot Grigio.

Enjoy!

KEFTA WITH POTATOES

For a summer day, a simple lunch can be very appreciated.

INGREDIENTS

- 1 pound of ground meat (I choose ground turkey, very lean)
- 2 to 3 garlic cloves, finely crushed
- ½ cup of finely chopped fresh parsley
- 1 tablespoon ground basil
- 1 tablespoon ground oregano
- 1 tablespoon ground cumin
- 1 tablespoon of Montreal steak seasoning
- ½ cup of olive oil
- 1 egg
- 2 to 3 potatoes, sliced lengthwise
- 1 squeezed lemon juice

PREPARATION

In a baking dish sprayed with nonstick vegetable spray, lay the potatoes to cover the baking dish.

In a separate bowl, put all together the ground meat, parsley, egg, olive oil, basil, oregano, cumin, Montreal steak seasoning, and crushed garlic. Mix all ingredients well to get a nice amalgam. Set aside.

In a different bowl, add some olive oil, garlic, parsley, and lemon juice. With a brush, lay this sauce over the potatoes and put in the oven at 350 °F for 30 minutes.

From the bowl with the ground meat, make hamburgers to your liking (as thick or thin as you like).

Take the potatoes from the oven and lay the hamburgers over the potatoes for about 15 minutes in the oven.

Serve hot with a glass of red wine or with a cold beer.

Enjoy!

MISCELLANEOUS

MOTHER'S MADELEINE RECIPE

I remember eating these madeleines as a child. My mother always had them ready for us to eat when we came back from school.

INGREDIENTS

7 eggs
large glass of sugar
large glass of flour
1 teaspoon of yeast or bicarbonate
handful of raisins
handful of roasted nuts in pieces
paper or aluminum molds

PREPARATION

Beat the whole eggs in a large bowl with the sugar. Gradually, add the flour, the yeast, or bicarbonate, whichever you use. Add the raisins and the roasted nuts.

Mix well the whole mixture and fill the molds.

Put in the oven at 325 °F for ¾ of an hour.

NOTE FROM THE AUTHOR

It will take me another year to complete this cooking book with so many more recipes because every day as I prepare dinner, I make and try a new recipe, which I will document for an eventual another cookbook.

I would like to acknowledge and thank the following:

My beloved mother, who for many years passed on to me her recipes

My wife, Dr. Marina, for being my inspiration and degustator

My son Dr. Kenneth J. Dery, his wife Debbie and my grandchildren Adam Abraham S. And Sophia Hanna for putting so much of their own time to help me and support me

My son, Alland B. Byallo, for his beautiful art design of the book and who share my passion for cooking and who is a senior consultant and advisor.

My son Dr. MarkAlain Dery and his wife Liana for their moral support

Without their help, this book would have never been completed and published.

Dr. Gabriel Dery

Index

CPSIA information can be obtained
at www.ICGtesting.com
Printed in the USA
BVHW022343231121
622388BV00001B/2